SEVENTY-FIVE

SEVENTY-FIVE

Best NBA Players and Teams
Rated by Statistician who has Seen
Games Since 1947
(League's entire 75-year history)

DAVE HEEREN

urlink
PRINT & MEDIA

1603 Capitol Ave., Suite 310 Cheyenne, Wyoming USA 82001
1-888-980-6523 | admin@urlinkpublishing.com

URLink Print and Media is committed to excellence in the publishing industry.

Published in the United States of America

Library of Congress Control Number: 2021922433
ISBN 978-1-68486-026-5 (Paperback)
ISBN 978-1-68486-046-3 (Digital)

21.10.21

CONTENTS

This book was written because its author attended NBA games during every one of the league's 75 seasons and created most of the statistical concepts in use by the league to this day.

The first TENDEX formula came into being in 1958. By that time, at the age of 19, I had become an NBA fan, attending New York Knicks games every winter at Madison Square Garden.

Before the 1961-62 NBA season, the Knicks hired me and early that season chose me as the team statistician. TENDEX often received attention from one of the four greatest players of all-time, Wilt Chamberlain. I remember how flattering it was to have Wilt looking over my shoulder and asking questions about his TENDEX stats.

Much later, from out of nowhere, in 2003, I received a phone call inviting me to a meeting with publishers working on a new basketball encyclopedia.

I attended the two-day event, and I believe the rejection at that meeting of my prime TENDEX formula and replacing it with a deficient formula (an outdated version of TENDEX) was the No. 1 reason for the encyclopedia's failure to find favor with many NBA fans.

Let's say I'm a big NBA fan picking up this encyclopedia in 2003 at a store during the same year as Michael Jordan's third and final retirement.

Chances are that I am going to look first at the stats of Jordan, the most popular player of his era. And I am going to put it right back down again, probably with an angry leer, when I learn that Jordan was not rated Player of the Year a single time in the encyclopedia's year-by-year database.

I am glad that I did not tell the encyclopedia's editor that the database chosen for the encyclopedia was based on a TENDEX formula. It was the only deficient formula among the two-dozen in my system. If I had told him, he might have mentioned TENDEX in the encyclopedia and I would have joined the encyclopedia's publishing staff as targets of Jordan fan ire.

The faulty TENDEX formula omitted the important divisor for positional rating and has not been used in any of my basketball books. Centers, forwards and point guards always, on average, rate higher than shooting guards. It was possible (and happened eight times) for the greatest shooting guard (Jordan) to lose out in the Player of the Year ratings to players less dominant at other positions, according to the deficient formula used in the encyclopedia. TENDEX actually honored the great Jordan three more times than his NBA contemporaries, who picked him five times as MVP.

Statistics, unlike book texts, could not be protected by copyright, and so the thievery was rampant. Bob Bellotti was the only statistician I am aware of at that time who didn't try to "borrow" stats from me, change them a tad and pretend he was the originator. Bellotti telephoned to ask permission for using the TENDEX formula he knew I didn't like and persuaded the editor that it should be used in the encyclopedia. I liked his candor and the fact that he wasn't one of the thieves.

There was a lot of plagiarism of TENDEX going on. It started with the stat system's initial national exposure via *The Sporting News* and a basketball magazine in the 1980's. This was followed by a series of five annual *Basketball Abstract* books. So much of what I wrote was published by nationwide sources that it was no problem for would-be plagiarists to rewrite my words and copy my stats.

Once, a "borrower" didn't even bother to rewrite. He just reprinted a segment of text that I had written. But, somehow, the thieves always seemed to foul up even worse than the single errant TENDEX formula because they just didn't understand basic statistical concepts.

With a sportswriter/friend, John Harris, we produced an annual TENDEX Draft Report which, during 30 seasons of computations from 1984 through 2013, showed TENDEX to be superior to NBA scouts by a ratio of five players (TENDEX winners) to three (winners for the scouts) overall.

For example, the scouts placed Jordan only No. 3 in the 1984 draft when he was the TENDEX decisive No. 1. TENDEX outdid the scouts on more than two-thirds of the super-elite players drafted during those years, including a perfect record (100%) for the first five players in the Jordan draft.

The better the players, the better TENDEX was at rating them. NBA scouts were earning millions of dollars when, for a few dollars, any fan (or NBA executive) could pick up draft ratings more accurate than those of the scouts by spending a few dollars for a TENDEX draft report..

By that time, TENDEX was being used, not only on the official NBA website, without being acknowledged as TENDEX, but also officially by the top professional leagues in Europe and Australia. They did credit TENDEX.

Some of them made changes in their versions of the TENDEX formulae. A European statistician told me, I think it was in the year 2000, that he was cutting in half the statistical significance of free-throw percentage in his version of TENDEX in an effort to protect Shaquille O'Neal, who was a horrible free-throw shooter.

I replied: "Why does the best player in the world need your protection?"

But even Shaq does not measure up statistically to any of the elite TENDEX foursome consisting of Jordan, Chamberlain, Oscar Robertson and LeBron James. The four are close enough by the numbers so that you can make an argument for any one of them.

Dave Heeren

CHAPTER ONE

A PERSONAL LOOK AT NBA HISTORY

It was the early days of my first job after university graduation. In January of 1962, I was sitting at my desk in New York City's Madison Square Garden studying basketball statistics when I became aware of a large person standing behind me.

"Are you rating the players? They told me it's what you do." A huge hand reached out with index finger pointing at a row of Philadelphia Warriors statistics on the page in front of me. "What's my rating?"

I noticed that the finger was pointing at the line of statistics belonging to Wilt Chamberlain, whose team would be playing that night in the Garden against the New York Knicks. At age 23, I was on salary with the Knicks to do what I most enjoyed: Statistical tabulations for the team.

I looked up and made eye contact with Chamberlain, who at that moment became the first NBA superstar to make my acquaintance.

I was reminded of dropping a 300-pound weight – Chamberlain's actual weight – in the saddle of a race horse and then shoving the horse onto a track and expecting it to defeat other horses that had 100-pound jockeys in the saddle.

Unlike the thoroughbred race horses, Wilt was powerful enough not only to carry all that weight, but to beat every other contemporary NBA big man running back and forth on a basketball court. He was a world-class quarter-miler besides having a feathery fingertip touch for rolling the ball into the basket when he had no chance to break through for a "dipper-dunk."

Wilt and I were about the same age, but I felt somewhat intimidated by the man who had the broadest shoulders on a rock-solid physique that I had seen. Even his slender legs rippled with muscle.

He was known as Wilt the Stilt because of the physical contrast between his huge chest and slender legs. But, if you looked closely while he was being guarded by No. 1 rival Bill Russell, it was clear that all parts of Wilt's body, even the legs, made Russell's look small. Wilt outweighed Russell by 80 muscular pounds.

The Boston Celtics concentrated a lot harder on helping out Russell in his matchup with Chamberlain than the Warriors did on the reverse project. Even so, Chamberlain nearly always won the statistical edge over Russell while the multi-talented Celtics usually won the games.

"Without even finishing the numbers I can tell you this much," I said to Chamberlain, "You are either the best or second-best player in the NBA."

Chamberlain, who was much more down-to-earth than you would expect from a man of his revered status, smiled. "Better than Russell?"

"A lot better than Russell," I said. "He's not one or two."

"You mean the Big O?"

"The two of you both are having seasons much better than anybody else in the league's history."

"Well, it's not much of a history. Only about fifteen years."

"I think the numbers you and Robertson are putting up will be targets of record seekers for a long time," I said.

Smiling, Wilt responded to a hand motion by one of the Warriors' coaches and turned to leave. On his way out to the basketball court he looked back and said, "Well, maybe this season it's my turn to be the MVP."

According to NBA records, it wasn't. Russell won the official award for one of five times he was so honored.

Robertson gained a slight edge over Wilt from TENDEX for MVP that season, even though Chamberlain was setting scoring records that haven't been challenged in the past 60 years.

The two ranked one-two in the league, according to TENDEX, for a record 10 years in a row. One or the other was ranked No. 1 by TENDEX for 11 years in a row. The split was Robertson six, Chamberlain five.

Russell, the best player on a team consisting mostly of Hall of Famers, was at no time the league's best player, according to TENDEX. But 11 times he was either the best or second best player on the league's best team.

As for me, I wouldn't have another one-on-one conversation with Wilt until 1998, one year before his death. But in the intervening 36 years, no one in the NBA exceeded or even equaled the seasons Chamberlain and Robertson had concurrently in 1961-62.

Actually, no one has to this day, although Russell Westbrook came close. He did have four recent Triple-Double seasons, but failed to match Robertson's scoring numbers or durability in terms of minutes played. Westbrook and Robertson are the only players to achieve Triple-Double seasons in the NBA.

Robertson maintained a cumulative Triple Double average consisting of 10.0 or more points, rebounds and assists per game during his first six seasons in the NBA. His record was amazing because he averaged about 30 points per game for those seasons and three of his best seasons had been spent in college.

The Big O had the first, second and third-best seasons of any player in the history of college basketball, according to TENDEX statistics and official NCAA stats. There was a decisive distance between him and a small group of players, one of whom was Chamberlain, who came next.

In a commendably logical decision, the NCAA decided to add the names of its annual Division One basketball players of the year to a trophy bearing the name of Oscar Robertson. His name is on the trophy three times.

Robertson probably could have averaged a triple-double, with 30-point scoring for at least nine, maybe 10 years in a row, if he had the opportunity to go directly from high school to the NBA, as did another super elite player, LeBron James. Robertson's sophomore, junior and senior seasons of college basketball with the University of Cincinnati were off the charts.

He was so good that the 1960 U.S. Olympic Basketball Team for whom he was the undisputed leader, became legendary not only for the ease with which it won all of its Olympic games, but, maybe even more so, for the clinics, featuring Robertson, that it was invited to conduct for awed players representing other national teams.

1960 was the year the international game of basketball grew to adulthood. Individually, Robertson was by far the best player on the U.S.A. team. In contrast to great U.S. teams of later vintage, every player on the 1960 team was an amateur.

Chamberlain averaged 50.4 points per game for the Philadelphia Warriors in 1961-62, the season during which we had our first conversation. No one else in league history has averaged more than 40 points per game for a full season, although James Harden envisioned doing so during the shortened 2019-20 season.

Harden wasn't playing as many minutes as Chamberlain did, so his points total for most of that season exceeded his minutes played, just as Wilt's had done. No other player has done this for a full season.

Why is it important to play big minutes as did Robertson, Russell and Chamberlain? You don't need TENDEX, only logic, to understand that it is better to have superstars on the playing floor than second-stringers.

But you don't want to have worn-out players on the court, either. Chamberlain and Robertson were unquestionably the most physically durable players in NBA history, in terms of minutes played per game and per season relative to the difficulty of their combined offensive and defensive assignments. Russell often was given the opportunity to take breaks at the defensive end of the floor when teammates had the ball, so his minutes played totals were deceiving.

Chamberlain's 1.080 TENDEX rating for the 1961-62 season remains to this day the best ever recorded in the NBA. The reason he was not the TENDEX MVP was that the positional average for point guards is lower than for centers. It is not reasonable to compare ratings for players at positions with different norms, so when the adjustment was made for position, Robertson came out on top by a narrow margin.

But were either of them really the greatest player of all-time? A full study will be devoted to answering this question in the next chapter, with updates in the final chapter of this book.

The TENDEX system has consisted of as many as two-dozen statistical formulae and has been used officially by nearly every major professional basketball league in the world. But how does it compute the greatest players and teams? And why has it been the most widely-used statistical system in the history of professional basketball?

AN ALTERNATIVE TITLE

This book might be more accurately titled, *Seventy-Four*.

I can't remember if I attended an NBA game in the league's first season of play, 1946-47. So I can't say for sure that I had direct exposure to the league for all 75 of its seasons. But I did listen to a lot of games secretively on my radio after going to bed, so I may have been the NBA's biggest elementary-school-aged fan.

I know I saw the Knicks play at least one home game the next season, during which I turned 10. My dad, who was an editor for the sports department of *The New York Times*, got dozens of professional sporting event tickets for me to attend with himself, another relative or friend from the time I was 10 until I graduated from the University of Delaware in 1961. It was while attending the university that the idea for TENDEX came to mind.

I had joined the staff of the college newspaper, *The Review*, and was the sports editor during my sophomore year, 1957-58. I was covering a basketball game – can't remember Delaware's opponent – when the thought occurred that scoring wasn't everything, maybe not even the most important thing for a basketball player to contribute to his team.

Delaware had a player who averaged about 18 points per game, He was chosen all-conference but it looked to me as if the only thing that interested him was shooting, and he didn't do that very well. He missed a lot more shots than he made.

Another player on the team scored less than half as many points, but from where I sat appeared to be a better player. So I began tabulating numbers during that game and continued doing so in games that followed. I kept track of total points, missed field goal and free throw attempts, rebounds and assists.

At that time the NBA didn't tabulate blocked shots, steals or turnovers, so I didn't, either. I am sure that if

I had, the disparity between the two Delaware players would have been even greater than my final numbers disclosed.

When I added up the points, rebounds and assists, and subtracted missed shots, the player with less points had a much larger positive number than the shooting specialist.

I wrote a story for *The Review*, and shortly after that a favorable assessment of my new system appeared in the daily sports column written for the largest newspaper in the area, *The Wilmington Morning News*.

It wasn't called TENDEX yet – did not even have 10 statistical elements – but my new system was just four years away from drawing personal interest from Chamberlain, New York Knicks star Richie Guerin and other NBA players.

THE 24-SECOND CLOCK

It was the 24-second clock that turned the NBA into a major professional sports league. Before the mid-1950s, when the 24-second clock was introduced, the NBA consisted of players many of whom were receiving so little income that their primary source was somewhere else.

It showed. Some of the players were tall but not athletic. They were not in the best physical condition and, from the way they played the game it did not appear that they took it seriously enough to do a lot of practicing. This was true of every team except the Boston Celtics, who did things right.

They selected the best players available to them in the player draft. When it didn't look as if they could get a player that Coach Red Auerbach wanted, they worked out a crazy deal. That's how they got Russell, who more than offset offensive limitations by becoming the greatest defensive player in basketball history.

Auerbach always managed to surround Russell with excellent offensive players. So, while Russell often lingered at the defensive end of the floor to grab a few precious seconds of rest, legitimate NBA Hall of Famers John Havlicek, Sam Jones, Bob Cousy, Bill Sharman, Bailey Howell, Tom Heinsohn and/or Frank Ramsey put up big offensive numbers despite often being outnumbered in frontcourt, five players to four.

The Celtics averaged close to 120 points per game for most seasons during the Russell era from 1957 through 1969. But Russell's value to the team consisted more in holding opponents to fewer points than adding to the big Boston totals.

During Russell's 13 seasons, the Celtics won 11 titles. But that team was so talented that there were times when Russell wasn't even the best player.

Havlicek was.

One year Russell almost blew the championship game with a turnover, but in one of the most famously announced plays of sports history, "Havlicek stole the ball!...Havlicek stole the ball!...Havlicek stole the ball!"

But this wasn't Russell's team or Havlicek's. It was Auerbach's. The man was a genius. I wrote a full chapter about him in a book entitled *The Sporting Stings*. He was the best judge of talent in the league, maybe ever, and that includes hundreds of scouts. He was the best coach and made the shrewdest decisions.

When he thought it would be a good tactic, he also became a con artist.

Russell, for example, could have been drafted by the same franchise that within a few years thereafter got Robertson and Jerry Lucas with territorial draft choices. (What a team that could have been!)

But Auerbach talked the (then) Rochester Royals owner into trading the 1956 No. 1 draft choice in exchange for a lower choice and monetary considerations including a week's revenue from an ice show. Auerbach also worked the St. Louis Hawks into the deal in order to assure the acquisition of Russell.

Later, as the Celtics' general manager, Auerbach made an equally shrewd move to obtain, according to TENDEX ratings, one of the top ten players in the league's history, Larry Bird. Bird had a better bottom-line career TENDEX rating than even Russell.

With Bird in mind, Auerbach talked the league's owners into approving the selection of a draft choice a year early. So when it came time for Boston to make a first-round draft choice in 1978, Auerbach picked Bird with the No. 6 overall choice. Bird, a college junior, according to NBA rules at that time, was not eligible to enter the league until 1979.

Boston's rewards for waiting a year were three more league titles, three MVP awards for Bird and general recognition of him even now as runner-up to LeBron James as the greatest all-around small forwards in NBA history.

James, it must be noted, has a slight edge over Bird on offense, according to TENDEX, and a significant one on defense. He is in fact a better all-around player.

Even so, Bird was a great player.

BASKETBALL BROTHER-IN-LAW

My brother-in-law, Dick Davies, was a summer camp protégé of Auerbach's at a resort in New York State's Catskill Mountains. In the daily selection of teams consisting of mostly NBA and AAU players, Auerbach nearly always chose Dick as one of the team captains.

I saw Dick outplay two of the best guards in college basketball to earn a spot on the U.S. Gold Medal Olympic Men's Basketball team in 1964. My leaping celebration with Dick at midcourt after the final game I have often, with tongue-in-cheek, referred to as the most professional moment of my career. I was, at that time, a sportswriter assigned to do a story about the game.

But I did more celebratory jumping than writing.

Dick, whose older brother Bob was an NBA Hall-of-Famer, told me years later that during one of Auerbach's basketball summer camps, he had offered him a spot on the Celtics' roster. Dick told me he was head-to-head a better player than K.C. Jones, who was the team's starting point guard (Bob Cousy had retired). But, even though he knew he would get a lot of playing time, it was a job Dick couldn't afford to take.

"Not enough money," he said.

Robertson, whose brain for the game was as far ahead of most players as Auerbach's was ahead of front-office personnel, turned out to be the man who changed the NBA's unfair fiscal structure. Robertson spent his first 10 seasons, woefully underpaid, with one of the weakest franchises in NBA history.

Cincinnati did win 52% of its games during Robertson's decade of play for the team even though for all of it, the Royals had either one or zero good complementary players with the Big O.

He was four years past his peak when he "escaped" the Royals in 1970, because of a monumental deal that he, as head of the player's negotiating committee, worked out with the league owners.

Then, in his first season with Milwaukee, despite the wear-and-tear on his legs brought about by numerous 3,500-minute seasons, he co-starred with Kareem Abdul-Jabbar on a championship team that, according to TENDEX, was one of the best in NBA history.

Which was team No. 1, according to TENDEX? Was it the Chicago Bulls' greatest team? Or the Celtics' best? The Lakers'? Or somebody else?

Read on to find out.

BARRY AND REED: GREAT OMISSIONS

Two players who were ignored by the NCAA at the 1964 Olympic Trials, even though they were better than every player chosen for the U.S. Team, later became NBA Hall of Famers: Rick Barry and Willis Reed.

Barry and his brother Dennis were fellow New Jersey natives who became acquaintances of mine while

I was covering the Miami Dolphins during the Shula championship seasons.

Reed later offered me a job in the front office of the New Jersey Nets, which I turned down because my family was enjoying life in Fort Lauderdale. At that time it was an idyllic location. There were times back then when you could find vacant places on a beautiful beach.

The TENDEX record of dominating the scouts in accuracy for the annual draft indicated that they could have helped the Nets make choices so good that they probably could have won numerous NBA titles. TENDEX outdid NBA scouts in rating elite players through the years by an average of nearly seven out of ten.

The preceding is an accurate statement, even though overall the TENDEX margin was about eight-to-five over the scouts. When it came to the very best players, TENDEX was incomparable.

To the NCAA, which oversaw what was supposed to be an amateur organization, Barry and Reed were fiscally incorrect. Reed played for a small predominantly black college.

Barry played for the University of Miami, which through the years, despite all kinds of NCAA harassment, won five – change a few blatantly bad officiating calls, one of which the NCAA did apologize for but did not correct, and it could have been eight – NCAA Division One football titles and three baseball titles.

But the collegiate alma maters attended by Reed and Barry had a singular weakness: Inability to generate money for the NCAA. Actually, I can't recall Reed playing in a televised college basketball game.

Barry's team wasn't on TV much, either, but during the Olympic Trials in 1964 the NCAA was taking no chances: High-level scuttlebutt had it that the NCAA had blackballed the two standouts, relegating them to bench-warming status in Barry's case and to obscurity for Reed on a weak squad that had no chance of being around for the final game that would determine the constituency of the actual U.S. Olympic team.

TENDEX has never posed any doubts about Barry's basketball talents, rating him the seventh-best college player of all-time.

But the NCAA made one terrible mistake. It failed to take into consideration what might happen if Bill Bradley, who, because of his well-politicized Ivy League stature, was assured of being chosen for the 1964 Olympic Team before the trials began, fouled out.

The only AAU team in the trials was underrated and reached the finals against the Bradley team representing the NCAA. Bradley was outplayed in that game by an AAU player, and did foul out in the final two minutes.

The NCAA was forced to insert Barry in the lineup as his replacement because Barry was the only other small forward on the team. The next time down the floor the crowd got a good look at a player who would go on to obtain All-Star Game and Championship Series MVP status in the NBA.

Trailing by four points, the NCAA team needed a basket to sustain even the possibility of winning the game. But instead of a basket, there was a missed shot.

All the AAU team needed to do to secure victory was box out and get the rebound. But Barry out-jumped everybody and slam-dunked the ball at the peak of his leap.

Biggest crowd noise of the game!

The AAU team won anyway. Five AAU players, including Dick, made the U.S.A. team that went on to win Olympic Gold.

Four years later, minus AAU players, who by that time had been blackballed through aggressive NCAA actions following the 1964 embarrassment, the U.S.A. team lost. That was when the NCAA itself began to come under scrutiny. I can't recall anyone expressing surprise when NBA players eventually replaced NCAA players on the U.S. Olympic Team.

FINALLY, KNICKS WIN!

Besides the only two titles won by the New York Knicks, led by Reed, Lucas, Dave DeBusschere and Walt Frazier, the 1970s were noteworthy for the final six of the American Basketball Association's nine seasons.

In addition to Barry, who, along with George Gervin, was next behind Julius Erving at the head of the ABA's nine-season all-star roster, the new league's top guns included Moses Malone, Artis Gilmore, Dan Issel and Spencer Haywood. All of them went on to stand out in the NBA.

After the collapse of the ABA in 1976, the NBA became fortified with former ABA stars and entered a golden age of performance during the 1980s comparable to that of the Auerbach-Robertson-Chamberlain decade of the 1960s.

Led by legitimate Hall of Famers Bird, Robert Parish and Kevin McHale, the Celtics added three more titles to achieve an amazing total of 16 in the 30-year span between 1957 and 1986. Auerbach was the common denominator in all 16.

Despite the Celtics' consistency, the team of the 1980s was the Los Angeles Lakers. The Lakers were led on offense by Magic Johnson, aging-but-still-capable Abdul-Jabbar, James Worthy and, equally important, on defense by Michael Cooper, versatile Byron Scott and A.C. Green.

The Lakers won five titles during the decade.

The 1990's were dominated by the play of the Chicago Bulls and team stars Michael Jordan and Scottie Pippen, plus Horace Grant, Toni Kukoc and rebounder/defensive specialist Dennis Rodman.

Jordan played for six NBA championship teams. He was honored by TENDEX with eight Player-of-the-Year citations, tied for the most with LeBron James. The NBA errantly reduced Jordan's official number from eight to five, and he did not earn best-player honors a single time according to a huge 2003 basketball encyclopedia database. The database, unfortunately, was based on one (the weakest) of 24 TENDEX formulae .

I never did like that formula and was pleased when Bob Bellotti decided to call it *points created* after politely asking me if he could use it. I am just now, 18 years later, confessing to be the originator of an inaccurate statistic.

But the overall accuracy of TENDEX remains intact, and so do 23 of the formulae.

Rodman was the NBA's greatest rebounder of all-time on the basis of how many rebounds he collected per opportunity (see chapter six). He was a member of five NBA title teams and was deprived of No. 6 when an official decided in the closing seconds of a championship finals game Detroit was leading by one point that an elbow by Abul-Jabbar connecting with the face of Bill Laimbeer deserved a foul call...against Laimbeer's face.

Hey, the face is part of the ball, that is, except when it is committing a foul.

Abdul-Jabbar sank two free throws. Lakers won.

If it weren't for the Bulls, the 1990s would have been remembered as a substandard decade in NBA history. Scoring, a predictable mark of NBA excellence, diminished to a post-24-second-clock low during Jordan's 20-month leave of absence in the mid-1990s.

In desperation for more offense, the league reduced the three-point shot distance by more than a foot and a half for the 1994-95 season, the second of Jordan's absence. But he did return late in that season in hopes of leading the team to another title.

Counting a reduction of 15 inches from the original 25-foot distance adopted by the American Basketball Association when it introduced the shot in 1967, the total reduction was nearly three feet. It was therefore too easy a shot to reward with three points because the ABA had carefully experimented before adopting the 25-foot distance.

The mid-1990's three-point distance was so short (less than two inches longer than 22 feet) that it should have been reclassified as a 2½-point shot.

NBA games were turned from athletic competitions into three-point shooting contests for two years before the original NBA three-point distance was restored. Even then, the scoring was down because there just weren't enough high-level players to fill out a 27-team league.

Disappointed fans squirmed in their seats because the athletic slam-dunks they had become accustomed to during the 1980s weren't happening very often any more.

The turn of the century was marked by Shaquille O'Neal's dominance (in more ways than one) of the low post. Led by O'Neal, the LA Lakers won three straight titles. Young Kobe Bryant, who later led the Lakers to two more titles, was an outstanding No. 2 player for the O'Neal Lakers.

Tim Duncan teamed with David Robinson to lead San Antonio to its first NBA title in 1999. Duncan followed that, after Robinson's retirement, with four more titles before completing a 19-season career of excellence.

Duncan's feat was made even more impressive by the fact that the Spurs were playing in what was considered to be a small market compared with the Lakers, Bulls and Knicks.

Small-market teams don't seem to catch many breaks from NBA referees, but the Duncan-led Spurs won five times, anyway.

For a San Antonio team to outdo the New York entry, 5-2, in terms of league championships was as remarkable as the number of overall titles won by the Celtics (17) and Lakers (16).

Duncan, one of the most intense and underrated players in NBA history, contributed to all five and was the best player on most of them.

2003 DRAFT: ANOTHER SCOUTING BLOOPER

NBA scouts correctly rated high school graduate LeBron James as the best player in the 2003 draft. But they incorrectly underrated the second best player in that draft, Dwyane Wade.

TENDEX rated Wade the No. 1 overall player in the 2002 draft (when he could have been drafted No. 1 because James was still in high school). In 2003, TENDEX still rated Wade the No. 1 college player.

Scouts ranked him at the bottom of the first round in his sophomore year, so low that he decided to play another season for Marquette University's team. They placed him in the middle of the first round as a junior when he was drafted No. 5.

I was told that the predominant thinking among the scouts was that Wade, who went on to set a career NBA record for most blocked shots by a shooting guard, was too small.

He was 6-foot-4, at least four inches taller than Allen Iverson, who must not have been considered too small, because he was chosen No. 1 in the 1996 draft. Iverson never led a team to an NBA title because his individual priorities and mediocre man-to-man defense did not bode well for team success.

In that same draft, scouts made another huge error by overlooking future Hall of Famer Kobe Bryant (five titles) until the 13th choice. Looking back on Bryant's career, he was arguably better than the No. 13 player in NBA history.

The only reason Wade was drafted as high as No. 5 was a Jordanesque workout with the Miami Heat, which at No. 5 was the first team that thought he was good enough even for a competitive workout.

Ira Winderman, a friend who was covering the Heat for the South Florida Sun-Sentinel at that time, told me the Heat were stunned by the Jordanesque talent displayed by Wade during that workout.

To this date, James has led NBA teams to four titles but could easily have been six except for key injuries.

Wade (three titles, probably should have been four) was the dominant player in the 2006 Championship Series with Dallas despite an illness that weakened him for a week and cost Miami the first two games. They won the next four as Wade averaged nearly 40 points per game – the Championship Finals record for a full series is two points lower than that.

Those four straight victories against a team that appeared to be better than Miami at four of the five positions, represented the best individual effort I ever saw in a Championship Series.

Wade's career TENDEX rating equaled that of the more publicized Bryant (but, hey, Kobe played in L.A.), and it was Wade's outstanding performance for the great

U.S. Olympic team of 2008 that helped James decide to play in Miami instead of New York or Los Angeles at that time.

Wade averaged nearly a point a minute in that Olympics. He posted by far the best TENDEX rating for the U.S. team despite his position, shooting guard, which has the lowest standard rating of the five positions.

Wade and Bryant were exceptional players whose talents demanded the ball.

During that Olympics, in which Wade played as backup to Bryant, he became friends with James.

James later joined the Lakers (after Bryant retired) and led them to a title. But not to be forgotten were the four years James and Wade were together in Miami, all of which ended with the Heat in the championship series to the dismay of league higher-ups.

Miami won two of the four and many Heat fans believe a 2011 title could have been easier than the two they actually won except for decisive injuries to both James (the entire series) and Wade (the last three games). Both played, but nowhere near their usual level, except for the first three games, in which Wade averaged more than 31 points per game. Miami won two of those three, despite James' struggle with a shooting-elbow injury.

GREAT PLAYERS: FINAL FOUR AND MORE

Closing this with historical perspective, James ranks with Jordan, Robertson and Chamberlain as the best four-some, by a wide margin, of all-time.

Top-dozen talents include James Harden, Kevin Durant, Bird, Abdul-Jabbar, Hakeem Olajuwon, Karl Malone and David Robinson.

Wade is in the same bracket with Duncan, Bryant and Magic Johnson within the top 15 players. Duncan officially is No. 17, but his clutch play (five NBA titles) demonstrated that he belonged no lower than Robinson, who, with the same franchise, overlapping Duncan's career, had slightly more impressive regular-season stats, but only one league title.

Popular Stephen Curry, greatest shooter in NBA history, isn't as versatile, durable or as strong on defense as the elite final four, but he's good enough to earn a spot above the midpoint on the list of the league's all-time best 75.

CHAPTER TWO

THE FABULOUS FOURSOME

I remember Bill Raftery. Our lives overlapped in more ways than one.

Both of us grew up in northern New Jersey at about the same time. In the 1970s I saw a few televised games played by Raftery's team, Seton Hall University. For a small school, Seton Hall nearly always seemed to win more games than it lost. I thought it was because of Raftery's coaching.

Raftery, at one time an all-state player, moved from the coaching ranks to that of TV announcer. He held a prominent place in CBS college basketball coverage for more than 30 years. But, of course, the thing I remember best was his annual coverage of the NCAA men's basketball tournament.

I can't recall the game Raftery was announcing, but I do remember that there was a delay and his cohort in the announcing booth asked Raftery if he would share with viewers his long-term perspective on the sport. First thing he was asked was to compare players from that era (it was around the turn of the century) with the past.

Raftery filled 10 or 15 minutes with his evaluation of the great players of the game, including Michael

Jordan (then in his prime), Larry Bird and the whole array of talented Los Angeles Lakers. He compared each with a star of the past.

Only once during that time did he hesitate. Asked if any contemporary player compared with Oscar Robertson, he shook his head and said, "Nobody is like the Big O."

This, I'm sure, drew negative reactions from many viewers, because almost every time I have brought Robertson's name into a conversation about great basketball players, it has been resisted with shoulder shrugs or snorts of displeasure.

Robertson's career in the sport was marred by other people's unfortunate, for him, decisions. After becoming the first high school player to lead a team from an all-black school to an overall state title (he did that two seasons in a row), he appeared to be on his way to Indiana University, where he would have become an icon overnight.

During my lifetime the Hoosiers always have been known for great basketball teams. But they missed out on three likely national titles by deciding *not* to recruit Robertson. I have heard an insider's explanation of why they did this but will not mention it here. It was a ridiculous reason having nothing to do with Robertson's character or playing ability.

Instead, he wound up with a then-little-known University of Cincinnati team. I worked during 1962 and 1963 covering the Cincinnati Reds' home games in Crosley Field while Robertson was challenging Wilt Chamberlain as the NBA's greatest player of that era.

My rating system, TENDEX, placed both Chamberlain and Robertson well ahead of the Red Auerbach-hyped Bill Russell.

Everybody knew who Chamberlain was. He had excelled for an outstanding Kansas University team. Hardly anyone, even indifferent Cincinnatians, knew that Robertson, according to TENDEX, had achieved the Nos. 1, 2 and 3 greatest seasons of any college player.

WAS IT ROBERTSON OR ROBINSON?

My father-in-law, a native Cincinnatian, and a huge Cincinnati Reds fan, did not even know Robertson's correct name: Called him Robinson. I think he must have been confusing Robertson with the Reds' best player at that time, Frank Robinson.

Robinson was considered by me not only to be the Reds' best player but also the one who treated the media (myself included) with the most amiability and respect. He gave me a nickname and I enjoyed hearing him call me Highpockets.

But, we are talking about the greatest basketball players and I have decided to include Robertson in the conversation. Along with Chamberlain, Michael Jordan and LeBron James, Robertson is one of the four greatest of all-time.

Nobody else is close to these four, according to TENDEX or any other rational analysis of NBA history.

The prime-decade TENDEX value ratings of these four all are significantly higher than the best of the rest. Value Rating is the most accurate and the most comprehensive of the two-dozen TENDEX formulae.

At this point in NBA history, every fan is familiar with the exploits of Jordan and James. Both have received plenty of publicity, in Jordan's case for the past 30 years, in James' for the past 18.

So, for the sake of establishing credentials for Robertson and Chamberlain equaling the overwhelming present attention given to Jordan and James, I have been talking mostly about Robertson and somewhat less about Chamberlain whose exploits are better remembered than Robertson's.

Chamberlain's name is known by most contemporary fans, but often mistakenly is mentioned after Bill Russell. Wilt outplayed Russell consistently in head-to-head matchups.

Robertson has fallen so far behind the other three TENDEX finalists in NBA journalism that he is due for a lot of catching up. Jerry West and Elgin Baylor, Lakers whom he dominated in individual matchups, both have received at least as much if not more respect than Robertson.

West and Baylor were big-market Los Angeles Lakers.

Robertson played for the NBA's wee markets in Cincinnati and Milwaukee.

Robertson hasn't left the competitive starting blocks yet in honored comparisons with the two Lakers and even Chamberlain. Wilt played in the strong Philadelphia market before wrapping up his career in Los Angeles as a teammate of West. He also achieved popularity during three seasons in San Francisco.

Playing with broken bones in both hands, Wilt was named MVP of a championship series won by the Lakers. He also won a title with a Philadelphia team when the Boston Celtics had so much depth of talent that they were winning almost every year.

For these reasons, a challenging task has been justifying Robertson's place among the final four. We won't get much opposition to the other three, but most basketball fans I know want to downgrade Robertson or ignore him.

Problem for every Robertson critic I know: None of them actually saw him play during his prime between 1957 and 1966.

GREATEST HIGH SCHOOL PLAYER?

In rating greatest basketball players, let's start with the beginning, that is, high school basketball. Robertson was so good in high school that an Indianapolis couple, friends of mine, later told me with straight face that, while dating, one of them would often say to the other: "Let's go see the greatest basketball player in the world."

I laughed whenever one of them said this, but they were serious. And they were talking about Robertson when he was still in high school.

I did research on the greatest players in the world during the mid-1950s when Robertson was in high school. The best point-guard name I could come up with was Bob Cousy, later an NBA Player of the Year.

I saw Cousy play many times during the 1950s. Robertson was so much better than Cousy when their prime seasons overlapped that he dominated him in their only two matchups that I know about. After those two, Celtics' coach Red Auerbach wisely decided not to allow Cousy to play head-to-head against Robertson.

I could not imagine at any time after the Big O reached physical maturity at the age of 18 or 19 when Cousy could possibly have been as good as he was.

By the time I was finished with this line of research, I realized it might be true: Even in high school, it is conceivable that Robertson might have been the best player in the world.

As a college freshman, he was a versatile 30-plus scorer who often led the Cincinnati freshmen to such big leads that he was removed early from games in which he could have scored 40 or 45, in addition to the big totals of assists and rebounds that he always seemed to accumulate.

By the time he graduated from college, most of the basketball world stood in awe of him. He was the team leader of the all-amateur U.S. Olympic Team in 1960. That team was so good that it was invited to tour Europe putting on clinics for the best talent on the continent.

Always it was Robertson who ran that team, but he had excellent teammates. These included Jerry Lucas, Jerry West, and Walt Bellamy, all of whom were collegians at that time who went on to be Hall of Famers in the NBA.

Years later, when John Wooden was asked to speak in honor of the MVP of an all-star game featuring the best high school seniors in the U.S.A., Wooden made the comment that the game's MVP, LeBron James, was the "best high school player since Oscar Robertson."

Wooden's comment meant he was skipping a lot of great players, including members of the 10 NCAA champion UCLA teams that he coached.

Ask Wooden's greatest players, or, for that matter, a lot of other long-term basketball fans, especially New Yorkers, who was the greatest high school basketball player and many of them will name Kareem Abdul-Jabbar. Some might even say Lew Alcindor, which was Abdul-Jabbar's pre-Muslim name.

But not Wooden, Alcindor's successful recruiter to UCLA: He didn't hesitate in skipping right past the man he called "my most dominant" player to name Robertson as the bottom-line man.

According to Wooden's comment, either Robertson, whom he often saw play in high school in the hoop hotbed of Indianapolis, was the greatest, or it was a flat tie between him and James. Take your choice, but there are not many serious ties in the sport of basketball. In this sport you go to overtime.

The fact that Wooden, who lived to age 99, did not mention Jordan or Chamberlain, two of the four finalists in the "TENDEX Tournament," did not diminish the greatness of these two. Both made rapid improvement during their seasons of high school and, in Jordan's case, also college basketball before becoming dominant in the NBA. But neither impressed Wooden (or Raftery) as much as Robertson.

GREATEST COLLEGE PLAYER?

This brings us to the college level. The trophy awarded annually to the best college player is named for Robertson. But that choice was made about six decades ago. It does not necessarily mean it would be named for him if everyone who played the college game between 1960 and the present were considered contenders. Politics always has been a vital factor in NCAA decisions.

Who was really the best college player?

James played no college seasons, but was Rookie of the Year as an NBA player during the year when he would have been a college freshman, if he had attended.

Jordan and Chamberlain both had junior seasons in college in which they more than doubled the standard TENDEX rating for players at their respective positions. Chamberlain's was the fourth best college rating of all-time (+108%).

Robertson had the top three college ratings, and all three were far above Chamberlain's best. For the three years combined Robertson's rating was +157%.

In fact, Robertson's sophomore season of college basketball was by far the greatest of any player of all-time. His sophomore season was statistically his best because after that he was almost always targeted for double and triple-teaming by opponents and his game had peaked by his college sophomore year.

Jordan and Chamberlain also often faced special defenses in college. But they didn't handle these defenses with as much ease as did Robertson, who seemed to have a genius for making the right play to score or find an open teammate near the basket.

Because of the crowd of defenders watching Robertson, there was often an open teammate within scoring range. Robertson invariably would find the open player closest to the basket or somehow work himself clear for a shot.

Robertson's college career standard TENDEX Rating of 1.001 for a minimum of three varsity seasons was not that much better than runner-up Bill Walton (.976). But the numbers make the comparison seem much closer than it actually is.

The standard (average) rating for a small forward (Robertson's college position) is .390 compared to .470 for a center. Thus, the top centers – Chamberlain (two seasons only), Walton and Abdul-Jabbar – all graded out with career college ratings of slightly higher than double the average for the position.

Robertson's rating was more than 2.5 times above the norm for small forwards. This is at least 20% higher than anybody else ever to play the college game, including the three superb centers.

Comparing TENDEX ratings with positional averages yields these remarkable career college numbers: Jordan +60.3%, Abdul-Jabbar +106.6, Walton +107.7, Robertson +156.7.

Larry Bird (+96.7) and Pete Maravich (+93.3) rounded out the first team of college players with Robertson, Abdul-Jabbar and Walton. The second team consisted of Jerry West +91.7, Rick Barry +88.5, Jerry Lucas +85.6, Ralph Sampson +84.9 and Elvin Hayes +83.3.

Chamberlain played only two college seasons, but in those seasons his rating was about equal to Abdul-Jabbar's and Walton's. So if he had played a senior varsity season, instead of a year with the Harlem Globetrotters, he might have ranked No. 2 overall behind Robertson. But the best he could have done would have been a distant runner-up.

Jordan was improving fast during his three seasons of college basketball. By his third NBA season he had reached full potential, and he stayed there for 11-plus years, not including the time he took off. We have therefore identified his prime playing decade, actually 11 calendar years, as 1987 through 1997.

TENDEX value ratings (the best TENDEX stat) honored Jordan eight times as the NBA player of the Year, tied for No. 1 in that category with James.

GREATEST NBA PLAYER?

So, although Robertson appeared to have been No. 1 at the high school and college levels, what about the NBA?

TENDEX stats show not only that Robertson averaged a triple-double for his first six seasons in the NBA but that in all six he had TENDEX value ratings of better than +60%.

Achieving a +60% value rating has been done only two-dozen times in NBA history. Robertson achieved one-fourth of those great seasons, most of any player, and he did it in consecutive seasons that statistically appeared comparably dominant to his three college varsity seasons.

If he had been permitted to turn pro at an earlier age, we could be talking about nine straight +60 seasons for him, which would be one-third of an expanding group of elite player ratings.

Nine for Robertson. No more than five for anyone else.

Triple-doubles including double figures in points, rebounds and assists in the same game were popularized by the TENDEX citations of Robertson. The NBA's usage of TENDEX began after Robertson's career was over, so triple-doubles are much more publicized now than they were while Robertson was playing.

Robertson, who, as far as I know, didn't even know the statistic existed, has relinquished his long-standing record total of career trouble doubles to Russell Westbrook.

Westbrook, of course, has made this record a target. And in games when he is an assist or rebound short, will seek it with determination during the closing minutes or even seconds of a game.

Robertson could have gotten a lot more than he did, probably including almost every NBA game he played, if he had made this a goal. Moreover, unlike Westbrook, NBA rules during Robertson's youth prohibited him from playing in that league until after the year when his college class graduated. This rule was effective even if, like Wilt Chamberlain, he skipped his senior year.

LeBron James exemplifies the benefits of a great basketball player skipping college. James has found it advantageous to have played in the NBA during all four seasons when he normally would have been playing college basketball.

James and Westbrook also have benefited from liberalization of assist rules making triple doubles much easier to achieve. The passes to back-to-the-basket players that registered NBA record-setting career assist totals for Magic Johnson in replace of Robertson, and John Stockton in place of Johnson, both were achieved on passes to teammates with their backs to the basket.

Assists were not awarded in the NBA on passes to back-to-the-basket players during Robertson's peak decade, the 1960s. The Los Angeles Lakers began awarding them at the outset of the 1970s and were followed during that decade by the other teams.

THE GREATEST VALUE RATINGS

Based on statistical trends, there seems little doubt that, if Robertson had been permitted to enter the NBA right out of high school, his first 10 NBA seasons would have been at the +70% TENDEX value-rating level, between 13 and 15 percents above the other three great players. His best was a record +89.1% in 1963-64.

Value rating is the best overall measure of an NBA player's performance.

The only other player with a +80% or higher value rating is James, who graded out at +80.6% in 2008-09. Only five players – our individual final four and Kevin Durant – have had seasonal value ratings of +70% or higher.

Value ratings are lower than basic TENDEX ratings because they include standard ratings for reserves for the minutes on the bench by the player being evaluated.

A poor emulation of the standard rating for reserves is now known as VORP and occupies a lot of space on basketball stat websites. The RP in VORP stands for Replacement Player. Problem with it is that it varies so much from player to player. It is a poor substitute for a carefully computed standard (average) rating.

An NBA player with a reserve like John Havlicek or James Harden – both of these players were reserves for several seasons – will have what appears to be a negative VORP rating, even if he is a good player because his replacement is a better player than he is.

The reverse also is true, and more often: In this case, usually for a bad team, a weak starter is made to look good by the performance of his RP, who is awful.

Statisticians who desire accuracy should use the TENDEX formula, not the VORP. Actually, the same could be said of most TENDEX formulae. They are carefully computed to be logical. Logic is at the heart of all effective stats.

We have been discussing TENDEX value rating and have mentioned Oscar Robertson's.

As far as the other three great players are concerned, Chamberlain exceeded +60% five times, Jordan four times and James three in seasonal value ratings at the NBA level.

Durant did it twice, Westbrook, Wade, Chris Paul, and Harden once apiece.

Overall, as it now stands, Robertson's value rating for 10 best NBA seasons, including four considerably below his college performance and first six in the NBA, still ranks No. 1 at +58.6. Chamberlain is next at +57.7, then James +56.1 and Jordan +55.5.

But it's close, and that's why we are splitting hairs. So far we have not found a reason to lower the placement of any of the top four, but Robertson's slim lead may be realistically expanded by those amazing college seasons that cannot be counted, although they were much greater than the final three seasons of the NBA decade that do count.

The NBA is at fault for discounting those years. It prevented Robertson, the man (he was 18 years old) by not allowing him to seek gainful employment in the league during four years when it is obvious that he might have been a great professional player.

Subtract James' first four NBA seasons from the overall picture, to equate his NBA career with Robertson's, and he loses a lot, too. But not as much as Robertson, whose game matured at about the same age, but whose numbers were superior.

Here's another factor to consider. The phasing out of Red Auerbach from the NBA scene during the 1980s may have caused NBA officiating policy to change. I'm speculating about some of this, but there is no question that the policy for making calls in plays involving the greatest players was reversed at that time.

During the 1960s, Auerbach argued for refs to make more calls against Robertson and, especially against Bill Russell's nemesis, Chamberlain. And so, ever pliable when it came to the persuasive Auerbach, they did.

This policy flattened out during the 1970s as Chamberlain and Robertson faded from the scene.

And then there was a reversal.

During the 1980s and 1990s, the refs became much friendlier to popular players such as Jordan, Magic Johnson and Abdul-Jabbar. Also, to competitive big-market teams such as the Lakers, Celtics and Bulls. The Knicks no longer were competitive.

The Lakers and Bulls each won a title with huge help from an obvious but ignored offensive foul by a superstar, one on Abdul-Jabbar, one on Jordan.

The worst was called against bad-boy Bill Laimbeer after his face got in the way of an Abdul-Jabbar elbow.

The one committed by Jordan was less flagrant (knocked a defender on his back with a shoulder-and-elbow to the midsection) but led to a decisive basket setting up the elimination of mini-market Utah. The Jazz was in good position to win a league title.

TO THE DETRIMENT OF CHAMBERLAIN

During the 1960s, rules were changed at the highest level to the detriment, especially, of Chamberlain. One change was funny, even though it was made in response to the serious issue of Chamberlain's athleticism.

Wilt became frustrated by his poor free-throw shooting in one game and decided on a sure way to make one. He stepped back a few paces, got a running start, launched himself from behind the free-throw line, leaped across the 15-foot distance to the basket and dunked the ball before his feet hit the ground.

NBA officials acted quickly with a rule banning dunked free throws.

However, the league did not respond at all to an issue that should have resulted in a suspension to Boston Celtic genius Red Auerbach.

Instead, league officials nodded their collective heads in 1968 when Cincinnati, because of a late-season injury to Robertson, was at risk of not making the playoffs. The Royals had won five out of seven from the Celtics in regular-season games Robertson had played, but were eliminated when Boston made it obvious that it was losing its final game of the season to Detroit on purpose in order to knock the Royals and Robertson out.

The Celtics preferred a first-round matchup with Detroit, a team they dominated. With a rested Robertson ready to return to the lineup, Cincinnati would have been favored to win a matchup with the Celtics because of the one-sided regular-season results between the two teams. The presence of Jerry Lucas, one of the two greatest teammates Robertson ever had, was a major factor.

With their No. 1 obstacle eliminated by what appeared to be what gamblers referred to as "throwing" a game, Celtics went on to win another championship.

I have digressed to say the last few things in order to show that while James and especially Jordan have profited from playing during an era favorable to superstars, it went the other way for Robertson and Chamberlain. This needs to be considered in final evaluations of the players because referee calls and rule changes affect TENDEX ratings.

There was clear statistical favoritism in Los Angeles to boost the assists total of Jerry West, who was a great shooter but not a skilled playmaker.

At the same time Robertson's totals were slashed by so much, especially during the four years when Abdul-Jabbar was his teammate, that it would have made more than 100 percentage points of difference in the Big O's seasonal TENDEX ratings for those four years.

This was not so, however, during Robertson's peak seasons that are being counted in his best decade (the best players have prime decades, with lower ratings at the beginning and end of their careers). Robertson was different in that he was a great player while still a teen-ager, so at least three of his prime seasons occurred before he entered the NBA.

But before Abdul-Jabbar, Robertson did not have a talented center to feed for easy baskets. At that time this was a non-factor and so Robertson's loss of assists is not being compensated for in these ratings. But it affected his career value rating to the tune of more than 10 percentage points, so we are talking about a final value rating of Robertson in the vicinity of +70% instead of +60%.

How do I know Robertson lost many assists? Well, the clearest indication occurred at halftime of a game Milwaukee was playing in Los Angeles early in the 1970's. After ten seasons in Cincinnati, Robertson went to Milwaukee and became a feeding machine for Abdul-Jabbar to pour in baskets from the low post.

At halftime, an announcer pointed out that Robertson had ten assists. They interviewed Robertson, who said: "If the official scorer in Milwaukee would do the statistics the same way, I'd be averaging 15 assists, instead of eight."

If true, this would have increased his TENDEX rating by about 150 percentage points. My computations show that, if not absolutely accurate, it was a reasonable estimate. On most of his passes leading to baskets by Abdul-Jabbar, Robertson was not being credited with assists, with the exception of games played in Los Angeles.

Reason for the no-assist decision seemed to be that Abdul-Jabbar often had his back to the basket when receiving a low-post pass. He would then turn and drop in an easy shot over the shorter opponent who was defending him. The stinginess on assists prevailed throughout the NBA, except for Los Angeles.

SELECTIVE SUPERSTAR FAVORITISM

Besides the favorable official scoring in Los Angeles, there is no doubt that the TENDEX ratings of players such as Jordan, James, Abdul-Jabbar and Magic Johnson were abetted by favorable refereeing while they were playing for big-market teams.

In James' case, this is not a factor because only at the end of his career did he sign with the Lakers. Those seasons are not among the ones included in his prime decade numbers used in comparison with other TENDEX Hall of Famers.

Next after the elite foursome on the TENDEX all-time list is a group of players in the +40's led by James Harden and Kevin Durant. According to TENDEX value ratings, Harden has been the NBA's best player in six recent seasons while building a career rating of +48.4, fifth best of all-time. Durant is next at +46.2, followed by Abdul-Jabbar, Karl Malone, Robinson and Larry Bird to complete the top 10.

Personally, I think Larry Bird at +39.1, Hakeem Olajuwon at +38.9, and Dwyane Wade 37.6, with exceptional play in three title seasons apiece, were better than Robinson +40.1, two titles but unexceptional Championship Series play. He averaged three points less per game in playoffs than regular season.

Tim Duncan (+34.2) had become San Antonio's best player by the time the Spurs were regularly winning championships and probably should be placed next to Robinson on the TENDEX all-time list even though the numbers give Robinson the edge.

The TENDEX numbers don't lie but neither do the number of league championships. Duncan was a greater clutch player than Robinson. His playoff stats were better than the ones he compiled during the regular season.

Robinson benefited from playing prime seasons during a decade (the 1990s) that had some great centers but, overall, was below average for the position. Robinson's statistical comparison with lesser players caused his TENDEX value rating to rise.

For the same reason – lack of strong competition – Bob Cousy often is overrated. The competition in the NBA during the 1950s when Cousy was a perennial all-league selection, was not nearly as good as it was a decade later.

Cousy achieved his reputation against weak point guards and never made more than 40% of his field goal attempts for a full season. His career percentage was .375. This is not a good number for any player for any decade of NBA history other than the first, before establishment of the 24-second clock.

I saw Cousy play many times and was not surprised when Robertson destroyed him at both ends of the floor in early matchups. In the 1961 NBA All-Star game, Robertson's first, he achieved a TENDEX rating of 1.147, one of the best ever for an NBA all-star. He held his defensive assignment, Cousy, to .182, even though Cousy was having a career-best season.

THE GREATEST SEASONS

Another intriguing statistic is the all-time list of greatest seasons by individual players. It shows why our final four players are in fact the greatest.

Robertson is the record-holder with six of the top 20 individual seasons of all-time and these, obviously, could not count his three incomparable college seasons. His best NBA season was 1963-64 when he set a record, so far unchallenged, with a value rating of +89.1. No. 2 on the list was James at +80.6 in 2008-09.

Plus-70 value ratings were achieved by our final four players and one other. Counting the record season, Robertson did it four times, four out of the top nine of all-time. Jordan made the list of nine twice and Chamberlain, James and Kevin Durant (2013-14, +71.0) once each.

Regarding +60 ratings, there are 19 appearances by our four best: Robertson six, Jordan five, Chamberlain five and James three. Besides Durant, who added a +66.1 rating in 2012-13 to his +71.0 a year later, Harden, Wade, Westbrook and Paul each topped +60 once.

Overall, our four greatest-of-all-time players dominated with 19 of the 25 best seasons.

These numbers are positional. Each player is compared with standard (average) ratings for his position. Thus, no benefit is given to players whose center or power forward position put them in an advantageous position for building high ratings with easy shots and rebounds close to the basket.

These are overall ratings for the positions played by these players, including substitutes. Robertson's and Chamberlain's durability, playing so many minutes that gave below average substitutes so little playing time, moved these two ahead of the other contenders, who did not have quite as much durability.

James, however, gets the title of greatest-player-of-venerable-age by leading the Lakers to an NBA title in his 17th season, 2019-20. He got that far, however, by NOT playing 3,500-or-more- minutes in some seasons as did Chamberlain and Robertson. Jordan also played a lot of minutes, twelve times topping 3,000, with a high of 3,311. But twice, when he became fatigued, he "retired" for two or three seasons and restored his leg strength.

Abdul-Jabbar's team, the Lakers, won titles late in his 20-year career, but by that time he was only a slightly-above-average player.

ANOTHER IMPORTANT FACTOR

Another factor that appears to favor Robertson already has been mentioned but should be repeated because of its importance. Assists were not tabulated in the NBA as they are now until after Robertson's prime seasons. He would have had raw TENDEX ratings between 100 and 150 percentage points higher for his final four seasons if assists were awarded then as liberally as they are now.

His raw ratings for the first 10 seasons probably would have improved by 50 percentage points, but so would the rest of the point guards in the league. This would have resulted in the positional standard being proportionately increased so that the value ratings would not change.

At that time there was more generous distribution of the ball by point guards than there is today. Robertson never had a standout center to feed for baskets while he was playing in Cincinnati.

In Robertson's top season he probably would have topped the .950 TENDEX mark. Only NBA centers, with much higher rating potential, have done that, with the recent exception of Russell Westbrook. But Westbrook did not play enough minutes to sustain a record-setting TENDEX value rating for his 1.000 TENDEX season. He was rested a lot and this encouraged the high rating. Fatigue is a discourager of peak performance.

Except in comparison with Jerry West, whose assists totals were proven through research to be exaggerated over point guards on other teams, I do not count the additional projections for added assists for Robertson. Reason for this is that all point guards in the league, other than West who was already benefiting, would have improved their ratings by a comparable percentage.

And the only reasonable way to compare players is against norms established by others playing the same positions.

Yes, Robertson's ratings would have zoomed when he was assisting back-to-the-basket Abdul-Jabbar at least a half-dozen times a game without receiving credit. But there wouldn't have been much difference between the benefits to himself and other point guards during his 10 prime seasons.

A player such as Abdul-Jabbar, who lost a lot of rating ground by playing 10 years beyond the prime he achieved during his first 10 NBA seasons, can be down-rated too much for hanging around too long. This is why I do not include any seasons other than the peak decade for overall player evaluations.

It has been determined that there really is a peak decade for human athletic potential. For most men, it is between the ages of 18 and 28.

Robertson was exceptional, however, in actually having acquired the mature basketball skills before his 20th birthday so that he could be considered at that time in his actual prime.

Robertson's NBA career spanned three phases. The first six years, with full body strength and mature skills, his performance was unparalleled. The next six, including the amazing all-around 1971 Championship

Series performance, were great by the standards of most NBA players, but not himself. The final two were mediocre by any standards.

But if you count those remarkable college seasons and the high school play as a senior for which we have the eye-witness word of John Wooden and two of my basketball-loving friends, we have evidence of elite play for 17 years, maybe 18 (if you count both of his legendary state high school titles).

To validate my suspicions of exaggerated assist tabulation in Los Angeles compared with other NBA cities, I computed all the numbers. Even without a natural point guard (Jerry West, the designated point guard, was normally a shooting guard) the Lakers were averaging five percent more assists than players on other teams.

If you figure that for road games the numbers would have been equal, and this is a reasonable assumption, it means that Lakers' official scorers were giving out at least 10% more assists than the others. Probably more, if consideration is given to the fact that the other teams in the league did have actual point guards.

By the way, I think this is a mixed bag. It is not to the Lakers'credit that they did something to their players' advantage that other teams were not doing. But it is to their credit that they showed the way for improving the standard for awarding assists to bring it to where it should have been all the time.

ACTUAL EVOLUTION: NBA STYLE

The NBA was evolving to a superior league while Robertson and Chamberlain were concluding their college years. By the mid-1960s' NBA competition was as good as it was going to get.

It is true that during later seasons there were a few more great players in the league than during the 1960s. But the talent was thinned out, especially during the weak 1990s, by having to be distributed to three times as many teams.

At this point in our evaluations, it is going to be hard to unseat Robertson from the No. 1 spot because three or four uncounted collegiate seasons were among his actual ten best. As has been shown statistically, these seasons, when Robertson was already no worse than one of the two best players in the world, improve his value rating from the high +58.6 to at least +70.

No matter what computations are introduced – and all of the important ones are in this chapter – nobody other than Robertson can be rated above +60.Whether Robertson can be rated as high as +70 is debatable, but in my opinion +70 is the minimum career rating for him, not the maximum. It is a conservative number when all factors are considered.

A critical factor: If Robertson's man defense was no better than, say, fellow point guard Allen Iverson's reach-in-and-watch-go-by technique, our final comparisons might get close again, whether or not we ignore the uncounted seasons (in college) that would push him up to +70.

Jordan, Chamberlain and James all were/are excellent defenders, so to clinch the issue for Robertson requires him to be almost as good as these three defensively, and that means very good.

It is a basketball fact that individual matchups are decided as much at the defensive end of the floor as the offensive end. Was Robertson good enough on defense to maintain his edge over Jordan, Chamberlain and James?

How good a defender was Oscar Robertson?

We have mentioned Robertson achieving a 1.197 TENDEX rating in his first NBA All-Star game while holding Cousy to a rating of .182. But was it a fluke, or was he always great on defense as well as offense?

Well, Robertson did a similar number on Jerry West in the 1966 game, routing West in every aspect of play to achieve a TENDEX edge of 1.120 to .091. And, oh yes, he ran all over Jerry Sloan in 1969, .966 to .000.

All-Star games during the 1960's were serious events but not as important as NBA championship finals. How did Robertson do in an NBA Championship Series matchups?

A heart-breaking injury to Robertson late in the 1967-68 season probably cost that Cincinnati team a league title. So, really, Robertson had no other shot for a championship until joining Abdul-Jabbar on the Milwaukee Bucks for the 1970-71season.

After distancing everybody during the regular season, the Bucks crushed Baltimore four straight times in the Championship Series, including a 19-point road victory. Abdul-Jabbar, who averaged about 35 points per game, was named the series MVP.

But consider this: Robertson, who averaged 23 points per game and did not receive any credit for at least 25 low-post entry passes to Abdul-Jabbar leading to baskets that should have have been recorded as assists, was the TENDEX Championship Series MVP. And this is without even counting the hundred-plus percentage points those missing assists diminished his TENDEX rating.

Here's why Robertson deserved MVP.

The basic TENDEX rating for Abdul Jabbar in the championship series was about .980. The opponent he defended against, Wes Unseld, scored and rebounded at his normal pace and his TENDEX was about .700.

Robertson chose to defend Earl (the Pearl) Monroe not because Monroe was easy to defend, but just the opposite. Always, when opportunity was present, Robertson welcomed the challenge of defending players who were headed for the Hall of Fame.

Monroe was a Hall of Famer. But, after a respectable first game, in which Robertson was not guarding him as closely as he did thereafter, Monroe disappeared. His TENDEX for the series was .377, below average for any shooting guard, even many reserves. It was 128 percentage points below Monroe's .505 career norm.

Monroe was a legitimate Hall of Famer who usually posted excellent numbers, but he shot miserably against Robertson's defense.

All of Monroe's offensive numbers were sub-normal, for him, but the big downer was field-goal shooting percentage. With Robertson in his face, Monroe's field-goal percentage for the series was below .400. It was down about 100 percentage points apparently because of Robertson's defense.

Comparing the two key positions, Robertson, whose TENDEX rating was .759 (even without all those assists he was not awarded) more than doubled the rating of the man he was defending. Abdul-Jabbar could only have equaled Robertson in that bottom-line category by holding Unseld to .490 or lower. He did not come close to doing that.

Another thing in Robertson's favor was the immediate improvement of Abdul-Jabbar when Robertson became his point guard. After registering an .801 TENDEX rating without Robertson's help in 1969-70, Abdul-Jabbar boosted his rating to .990 in the championship season, an improvement of nearly 25%. Kareem matched that with .992 the next season, Robertson's 12th and final all-star NBA season.

The first two seasons with Robertson were among Abdul-Jabbar's three overall best, only one of which occurred while he was playing 16 seasons with the Lakers.

I know, the custom is automatically to pass out awards to the highest-scoring players. But in this case numbers show that Robertson was the 1971 Series MVP, even though, as so often happened, he was overlooked for the honor he deserved.

At this phase of Robertson's career he was five years past his prime but still a superstar. Abdul-Jabbar, one of the top eight players of all-time, was smack in the middle of his prime.

So what if that was uncharacteristic? What other highly visible (TV and all) events were there in NBA history for which we still have statistics, other than Championship Series?

The answer to that is All-Star Games. We have mentioned several awesome individual performances by Robertson in these games, but here's the overview: Robertson was chosen to play in the game during his first 12 NBA seasons. His team won 11 of the 12, and in six of those, TENDEX showed that he had the best stats and, on that basis alone, deserved MVP honors.

He was awarded three of the six. Heck, as great as he was with hard-to-compute intangibles, including man defense, maybe Robertson was the winning difference in all eleven.

Or maybe the fact that he won 11 times was coincidental?

I don't think so.

PERTINENT MATCHUPS

One of the all-time great matchups in the NBA was Robertson against Jerry West, which had been the backcourt tandem for the dominant 1960 U.S. Olympic men's basketball team.

That is, for Robertson it was a great matchup. Not so much for West.

In All-Star game competition, when guarding West, Robertson held him to less than half of his regular-season scoring average while doing what he always did on offense, that is, dominating. The same thing happened a lot during their regular-season matchups, so let's not even consider the possibility of coincidence.

In those days the teams tried their best to win All-Star games. Players regarded as standouts were named starters and played as many as 35 or 40 minutes. West had his chances, but rarely was good enough to beat Robertson's tenacious defense.

Some readers may now be thinking about how West was named officially to the league's All-Defensive team more often than Robertson was. That goes right back to the marketplace. Big-market teams usually dominate all-defensive choices, which are often popularity contests rather than based on performance. Read on for support of this statement.

By playing for two of the weakest franchises in the league, Robertson was never to receive the honors he deserved. His limitation to one league MVP demonstrated that right off the top. TENDEX showed he should have won six. Make that 10, if Chamberlain had not been contemporary and Auerbach had not been awing sportswriters with legends of Bill Russell's pre-game puking.

The only thing Russell actually accomplished with his pre-game alleviations was to give himself plenty of space in the locker room.

Before the 1963 All-Star game, perhaps for West's sake, the Lakers tried to embarrass Robertson. They issued a public challenge for him to play head-to-head against Elgin Baylor to determine who was the best 6-foot-5 player in the world.

The Lakers thought the bulkier Baylor, who usually posted similar scoring numbers to Robertson's, would dominate the matchup because of his strength.

Robertson dominated because his NFL linebacker's prototype body proved to be superior to Baylor's. The Big O had quicker feet, and possessed a Jordan-challenging 40-inch vertical jump that turned a deficit on the boards into an advantage. An old photograph of Robertson grasping a rebound with his head within three inches of the basket rim proved the 40-inch capability.

For doubters, there is a way to prove or disprove this with simple arithmetic. Just add 40 inches to 77 inches (Robertson's height) and see how many inches short of 120 (10 feet) this places you.

The Big O gave evidence that he could have gotten as many rebounds as Elgin – that is, 15 or 16 per game during prime seasons – if he had played power forward regularly. NBA point guards have to stay on the perimeter much of the time to thwart opponents' fast-breaks, which is one of the reasons that they have lower TENDEX ratings than power forwards and centers.

Robertson was much more versatile in making plays for himself and teammates than Baylor.

And then there was that underrated, tenacious man-to-man defense: For one quarter he held Baylor scoreless. Baylor could not stop Robertson, who dominated on offense as usual.

As the second quarter began, Baylor went back to his normal power forward position. But the West never recovered from the nine-point deficit incurred while Robertson and Baylor were guarding each other. If they had kept on guarding each other, who knows? Could the East have won by 36 points?

We have mentioned Cousy. He was generally considered by far the best point guard to play in the NBA before Robertson. Cousy matched Robertson by winning one official league MVP award.

For the first two seasons of Robertson's career, his Cincinnati team played in the NBA West. This meant a Robertson-Cousy matchup when the two were chosen as point guard starters for the All-Star game during Robertson's rookie season.

This matchup was as one-sided as the Robertson-Baylor debacle. It seemed that the bigger, stronger, faster, smarter, better-shooting Robertson was simply in a different category from Cousy as a basketball player.

And this happened when Cousy was in the middle of achieving a personal-best TENDEX rating for a single season. He was in his prime.

After the first two seasons playing for the West team, Robertson played for the East team eight times, winning seven against the likes of West and Chamberlain. He closed out with two games on the West team, both victories.

The only loss for whichever team Robertson was a roster member happened in the 1967 game when he was on the East team while Rick Barry was scoring 38 points in 34 minutes for the West.

Barry was not being guarded by Robertson, but I would have liked to see what a Barry-Robertson matchup would have been like when both were in their primes as they were at that time.

No. Robertson would not have shut him out as he did Baylor. Barry was quicker, had more ball skills and more shooting range than Baylor.

But it would have been worth seeing.

John Havlicek, an excellent defender often given the Robertson assignment by Auerbach after the Cousy disaster, said this about the Big O: "When he dribbles it looks as if the ball is magnetized to his hand. It always seems to come right back to that hand."

Robertson was not just a good defensive player. He was a *great* defensive player, and a *great* offensive player, the only player I have seen whose greatness was evident at both ends of the floor.

As far as this NBA observer is concerned, personal opinion has been affirmed by TENDEX, and we have settled the question of who was the greatest NBA player of all-time.

His name is Oscar Robertson.

CHAPTER THREE

GREATEST NBA TEAM: SURPRISE!

Historically, the NBA has been a league of hype emphasizing popular players on teams linked to franchises generally recognized as the elite. And so, whenever comparisons are made between the league's greatest teams, it usually comes down to a dialogue involving a few representing prestigious markets.

You'll hear advocates for all six of the Chicago Bulls' teams of the 1990s, for the five won by the Los Angeles Lakers between 1972 and 1988. And, take your pick, from any of the championships won by the Boston Celtics after 1960. Or the Golden State Warriors three between 2014-15 and 2017-18

The dividing line is 1960 because that was the year the U.S. Olympic Team matched up well against the NBA All-Star team. The top four Olympians that year probably equaled or surpassed the best four players already in the league.

The league at that time did not have a single guard even close to as great as newcomer Oscar Robertson. Based on statistical evidence presented in chapter two, Robertson was so exceptional at both ends of the floor that he probably was the best player in the world at that time.

The NBA was a vastly superior league after 1960 Olympians Robertson, Jerry West, Jerry Lucas and Walt Bellamy entered the league than before. And, so, in reality, even though Lucas didn't come into the league at that time, it matured that year. Before 1960 there were no NBA teams comparable to the Hall of Fame dominated roster of the nine 1960s champion Celtics teams.

After being stuck for a full decade on the roster of one of the worst franchises in NBA history, Robertson found an excellent team to play for during his declining years. That team, the Milwaukee Bucks, won a championship in 1971 with a 4-0 Championship Series sweep of the Baltimore Bullets. None of the four games were close.

Is it possible that could have been the best team ever?

The perennially mediocre New York Knicks made their diehard fans, including me, ecstatic by winning two league titles early in the 1970's.

Statistically, those Knicks teams were very good, but don't use any word other than *great* to describe them in conversation with New York sports fans. The 1969-70 Knicks met our qualifications by winning both regular season and playoff honors and had a lot of supporters, at least in New York. as the greatest team of all.

You won't hear much support for the San Antonio team that won five titles with Tim Duncan, beginning in 1999. But, on average, those teams were statistically better than the two Knicks championship teams. The Spurs were not saddled with as weak a starter as political Bill Bradley.

Few people will complain if you don't even bother mentioning the Bullets' team that came back after losing four straight to the Bucks in 1971. They moved to nearby Washington and won a league title in 1978 with Elvin Hayes joining Wes Unseld at the power positions.

Yes, I know, Washington is the nation's capitol. But it has more politicians than serious basketball fans. It is probably the team for which Bradley would have have felt most comfortable playing for.

So let's get serious: The greatest of all NBA teams, according to many pundits woking out of the league home office in Madison Square Garden, probably called New York home. But we definitely can't rule out Los Angeles or Chicago.

Boston or Golden State? Maybe, maybe not.

But should we listen to the an argument for including Detroit and Philadelphia to make five contending franchises out of a total of 30?

According to the line of thinking I believe is prevalent around the NBA, we should discount all of the so-called little guys, if there is such a thing in professional basketball.

Sorry, but we can't do that. The top teams of all-time, according to TENDEX, included at least three not on anybody's big-market lists. Make that five, if you include the two recent Golden State teams that won both regular-season and playoff honors. Those teams, with 67 regular-season victories in each, were among the top dozen of all-time.

Golden State had a third league title and a record-setting 73-victory regular season, but in neither of these years did the Warriors win both playoff and regular-season honors, which is the initial qualification for consideration as the best of all-time.

It's difficult to conceive of a team claiming the title of all-time greatest without having won the league championship. Or without proving itself best in a regular-season schedule of 80 or 82 games.

Had the Warriors won the league title after the 73-victory regular season, that team would have ranked, according to sophisticated TENDEX formulae, among the top three teams, possibly as high as No. 1.

Golden State was not considered a major market until the recent success. Neither was San Antonio before its five championship seasons within the past 22 years.

Ruling out bias of any kind means we must consider any champion team that meets the two basic criteria, no matter how big or small the market.

DECADE OF GREATNESS

The NBA maintained a tight average size of less than ten teams through the decade of the 1960s, and this assured the greatness of that decade from the team standpoint. There were plenty of excellent players at that time in the league to stock nine teams.

By the end of the '60s more than half of those teams were becoming good enough to contend for the league title. This was when the competition really got good, not when the Celtics were dominant, but immediately after that.

The decade of the '70s, which began with a 17-team league, was remarkable for the fact that eight teams won championships. The Celtics and Lakers won two apiece. It was a very well balanced league.

Predictably, the best of those teams, the 1970-71 Milwaukee Bucks, was not even mentioned as a contender on the last greatest-NBA-team poll I remember seeing. There was no way any team from a city of suburban size should ever be compared with the Knicks, according to prideful insiders.

I am going to agree with them on this. There is no way the Bucks' championship team should ever be compared with the Knicks' best team. The Bucks, with a superior starting unit and a better bench, was clearly the superior team. Statistics compiled during a comprehensive analysis support that conclusion.

The Bucks took such a big lead over the pack in 1970-71– largest in NBA history – that their No. 1 seed in the playoffs was decided about a month before the end of the season. The Bucks started preparing for the playoffs and losing concentration on meaningless games when their TENDEX rating was 114.8, best of all-time. The Knicks of 1969-70 played at a pace equivalent to a rating of 108.7.

In other words, the Bucks were more than six points better per game than the Knicks' team of the preceding season. They were between three and four points better per game than the second and third-ranked teams, the Golden State Warriors of 2016-17and the Chicago Bulls of 1995-96.

I must admit that as a Knick fan from elementary school, I did not agree at first with this conclusion. But it was supported by every one of the relevant TENDEX formulae. The Bucks were simply the better team.

Actually, they were the best team ever to play in the NBA during its first 75 seasons. TENDEX gives evidence to that, and so does the lack of competition for the Bucks that season from any of the other seven teams that won titles during the decade.

For the 1995-96 Bulls and the 2016-17 Warriors the overall ratings combining regular-season and postseason were so close as to be indistinguishable. Let's call it a tie for the second-best team of all-time.

But the 1970-71 Bucks were decisively No. 1.

Here's why.

That Milwaukee team finished a record 14 games ahead of the second-best team that year even though Oscar Robertson and Kareem Abdul-Jabbar spent much time on the bench during the final six games. The Bucks lost five of those six, but didn't care.

At the rate they were going, winning every game near the end, they could have achieved an unchallengeable record by finishing 19 games ahead of the next best team.

In a 162-game schedule, such as is played in baseball, this would have been equivalent to finishing 38 games ahead of the second-place team. There never has been a finish even close to this lopsided in a baseball season.

If not for losing those five restful games at the end that they probably could have won, the Bucks hypothetical 38-game advantage for a baseball-length season was reduced to an edge of "only" 28 games.

But it effectively eliminates the 2016-17 Warriors from any sort of contention. They concluded their regular season with a six-game edge over San Antonio.

All three teams were dominant in the playoffs. The Bucks were most dominant with their four-game rout of the Bullets in the Championship Finals.

Even though the Bucks' regular-season TENDEX rating was diminished from 114.8 to 112.8 by the indifferent finish, they still ranked No. 1 of all-time in that category.

The average NBA team has a rating of 100. This translates into a 15-point underdog role against the 70-71 Bucks on a neutral floor in a game the Bucks were trying to win.

What Milwaukee got from the final six regular-season games was important rest for Robertson and Abdul-Jabbar. Both played some of their finest basketball in the Championship Series.

THE UNDEFEATED HALF-SEASON

The Bucks mounted a 19-game winning streak before the season-ending respite. Earlier in the season, they had a winning streak even longer than that one.

The two streaks combined represented a half-season undefeated for the Bucks.

And this was during a much more difficult era to compile winning streaks than the present, e.g., the Warriors' four-season supremacy. It was difficult because the full schedule was completed in a shorter period of time.

One of the most impressive feats of that Milwaukee team was a four-game winning streak…in four days.

If it meant anything to the Bucks, the team could have won 70 or 71 games and challenged for the No. 1 spot all-time in that category if it had any interest in doing so.

Obviously, it didn't.

All Robertson and Abdul-Jabbar wanted to do was win, and their collaboration, in Robertson's first season with a strong team, resulted in a memorable championship performance.

We have seen that TENDEX value ratings give a big edge to Robertson as the greatest point guard of all-time and supports him as the best player at all three levels of competition: high school, college and pro.

Even though he was past his prime in 1970-71, his play that year was perfect for team needs. Under today's rules, he probably would have averaged at least 15 assists per game. Entry passes to back-to-the-basket Abdul-Jabbar leading directly to easy shots for field goals would have been counted as assists.

But even without counting the omitted assists, which would have pushed Robertson's TENDEX rating close to .900 for the Championship Series, the lesser statistics still showed him to be the best player in the series: He averaged 23 points and shut down Hall of Famer Earl Monroe, Baltimore's best all-around player.

Abdul-Jabbar, the league's second-best center of all-time, according to TENDEX, was in his prime. And so was small forward Bob Dandridge, who averaged 18.4 points and whose career TENDEX rating for the small forward position was much better than that of super-hyped James Worthy of the Lakers.

Moreover, Jon McGlocklin, the Bucks' shooting guard, had one of his best seasons with 16.8 points. And Greg Smith and Bob Boozer combined for more than 20 points and 12 rebounds from the power forward position.

This team had several good players coming off the bench, headed by Boozer and Lucius Allen.

The Chicago Bulls of 1995-96, posted a TENDEX rating of 112.2 and won 72 games, but we have seen that in reality they were not as close to the 70-71 Bucks as the final ratings made it appear. Chicago that year was intent on breaking the league record for victories and tried hard to win every game, even meaningless ones at the end. The middle seasons of the 1990s in the NBA were not nearly as deep in strong teams as were any of the seasons during the 1970s.

The Warriors of 2016-17, with their best player of this era, Kevin Durant playing his first season with the team, produced a TENDEX rating of 111.2 and 67 victories. But this team, like the 1995-96 Bulls, did not face very strong opposition.

At times, it seemed that the LeBron James-led Cleveland Cavaliers were the only respectable opponents for the Warriors. The Cavs did interrupt the run of three Golden State titles with a Championship Finals upset over the 2015-16 Golden State team, which had won a record 73 regular-season games.

In 1970-71, every team in the Bucks' Midwest Division won at least 45 games, but Milwaukee finished

15 games better than the Bulls, who placed second in the division.

The four teams in that division posted the best overall record for a division in league history with 210 victories and 118 defeats. You didn't need TENDEX to figure that for a .640 winning percentage.

The Bucks went 14-1 in that division. They won their first two playoff series by 4-1 margins before taking four straight from Baltimore in the championship series. This is sound evidence for the Bucks dominance over strong competition.

How much better was that Milwaukee team than the rest? Well, there were four best-of-seven playoff series that did not involve the Bucks. Three of the four were extended to the seven-game limit.

BULLS AND WARRIORS: STRONG, TOO

And yet, the 1995-96 Bulls and 2015-16 Warriors were very good teams, certainly good enough to rank No. 2 and 3, respectively.

Dennis Rodman, the only NBA player ever to post a career average of pulling down more than 20% of the available rebounds during his minutes on the floor, impacted the Bulls team almost as much with his defense as Jordan did the offense.

The 95-96 Bulls also featured small forward Scottie Pippen, a better player than Dandridge, although both were TENDEX Hall of Famers. And then there was super sixth man Toni Kukoc and guard Ron Harper, who at one time early in his career appeared to be a sure Hall of Famer.

Although slowed by major knee injury while attempting to emulate Robertson with a single season averaging 45 minutes per game for the Los Angeles Clippers, Harper was a good backcourt teammate for Jordan.

Both were natural shooting guards. Officially, Harper was listed as the point guard, but the Bulls made sure Jordan handled the ball a lot more than Harper did. This made Jordan, in actuality, the point guard, but you should have heard the screams of horror when this was pointed out to a Jordan adorer.

Is it a bad thing to be able to play three positions with regularity as Jordan did? Late in his career he played a lot of small forward.

Or four positions, a unique accomplishment by LeBron James?

As great as the 70-71 Bucks were, they could not have ranked higher than the 95-96 Bulls, if not for the center position. Abdul-Jabbar was in a different time zone from Chicago's so-so starter, Luc Longley.

Robertson and Abdul-Jabbar were the difference makers. Golden State star Stephen Curry, who often struggled against Cleveland's Kyrie Irving, did not have the ball-handling skills to free himself for good shots against the man defense of Robertson, nor did he have the strength or mobility to guard Robertson effectively.

The Warriors, like the Bulls, would have struggled mightily in the post where Abdul-Jabbar, the league MVP that year would have been matched by a rotation of three pretty good, but not great, big men.

On the other hand, the Warriors would have had the edge at small forward with Durant and at shooting guard with Klay Thompson. But that edge would not have been as large as the advantage earned by Abdul-Jabbar and Robertson at both ends of the floor.

WHAT ABOUT BASEBALL AND FOOTBALL?

To place the Bucks' 70-71 season in perspective, it was probably the most dominant season by any team in the history not only of pro basketball, but also baseball and football.

I was an intense New York Yankee fan during the career of Mickey Mantle, when the Yankees were near their all-time best year after year. In the first 12 years of Mantle's career they were comparable to the 1960's Celtics, in large part because Mantle was both the strongest (600-foot-plus home runs) and fastest (3.1 seconds from home to first base) player in baseball history.

But except for 1961, when Mantle was unable to finish the World Series because of an errant medical procedure, the Yankee champion teams were never as dominant as those of the Bucks.

The '61 Yankees probably were as talented, comparatively speaking, as the 70-71 Bucks. But, even though they won four out of five from Cincinnati in the World Series, that team was not nearly as good as it could have been with Mantle healthy.

The Yankees probably fielded their best team in 1960 with Mantle intact. But the Pirates won that series

4-3 even though the Yankees more than doubled their runs scored total for the entire series.

Take away aging manager Casey Stengel, fired after that World Series because of numerous bonehead decisions, besides often falling asleep in the dugout, and maybe that Yankee team would have won four straight, as it probably should have done.

But it was not a better team than the 1970-71 Milwaukee Bucks.

I covered NFL football before and during the 1970's when the league peaked with consistently outstanding Green Bay, Dallas, Miami, and Pittsburgh championship teams. None of those, in my opinion, were as dominant as the 70-71 Bucks.

Besides having two of the top half-dozen players in league history, the Bucks were good at every other position. They had no weaknesses. The Bulls and Warriors had gaping holes at the center position.

I never saw an NFL or MLB team that had no perceptible weaknesses.

To qualify as a finalist in the greatest-NBA-team sweepstakes, a team must have won a league championship and posted the best won-lost record of the regular season, in other words, a regular season championship.

The Bucks not only took four straight in the Championship finals over the Bullets, but also posted the best team TENDEX rating of all-time and the biggest regular-season victory margin against very strong competition. They were truly dominant.

CHAPTER FOUR

CALL THEM THE SHOOTISTS

The formula for shooting efficiency (Shootist) is one of the simplest on the TENDEX list. Instead of having ten or more components, like most of the others, Shootist has only two: Points per shot.

That is, total points divided by total shots.

This is a much more important statistic than scoring average. We have seen that in the earliest days of the NBA a player (Joe Fulks) led the league in scoring in 1947-48 when he took so many shots a miniscule 25.9 percent of them went in the basket. We are not including three-pointers. They didn't exist until 30 years later.

In this book individual total points are not considered important enough for commentary or charting. It isn't about scoring. It's about shooting. The best shooters are more valuable to their teams than the bulk scorers.

A few regular players with careers spanning ten or more seasons have averaged at least one point per shot. However, only one has averaged more than 1.1 points per shot: Stephen Curry.

As far as pure shooting is concerned, no one is better than Curry.

No one is even close to as good.

When you add up his total points via two and three-point field goals and free throws, and then divide by total shots from the field and free throw line, the bottom line number is 1.116.

The next best regular player I have found is Kevin Durant at 1.029.

Curry has been a lot better than that during his (so far) 12-season NBA career. His career percentages are .907 (free throws), .519 (two-point field goals, twice as good as Fulks), and .433 (three-point field goals).

The 2020-21 season was one of Curry's best. He averaged a career-best, league-leading 32.0 points per game. His individual percentages were .916 (free throws), .569 (two-point field goals) and .421 (three-point field goals).

Curry's 2020-21 season was reminiscent of Michael Jordan's great 1995-96 season. After nearly a two-year absence from the game, Jordan came back strong. His game, which had fallen off slightly during the tiring drives to three league championships in a row, was restored.

He had one of his greatest seasons with fresh legs and launched another string of three championship seasons in a row with help from excellent teammates.

Curry didn't "retire" but an injury sidelined him for all but five games during the 2019-20 season. He came back with fresh legs and had his overall best season in 2020-21. It is interesting that this great season for Curry was one of the worst for the three-time NBA champion Warriors since he joined the team. They failed to make the playoffs.

I have not done points-per-shot statistics for every NBA player, but I did do so for those known to be excellent shooters. The leaders are below, those who have averaged better than one point per shot:

1. Stephen Curry, 1.116
2. Kevin Durant, 1.029.
3. Kevin McHale, 1.026.
4. Reggie Miller, 1.025
5. Kiki Vandeweghe, 1.023
6. James Donaldson, 1.022
7. Kareem Abdul-Jabbar, 1.021
8. Bobby Jones, 1.017
9. Brad Davis, 1.016
10. Larry Nance, 1.013
11. Danny Ainge, 1.011
12. Jerry Sichting, 1.009
13. Darryl Dawkins, 1.008

An explanation is required for the rating of Miller. If you count his three-point shooting during the three seasons (1994-95, 95-96 and 96-97) when the line for that shot was reduced to about 22-feet, his rating is 1.031, a couple of points higher than Durant's.

The reason for the adjustment should be obvious: The three-point shot was much easier during the middle years of the 1990s than at any other time.

Another player who benefited was Michael Jordan. He had been a mediocre three-point shooter until that time, but became a pretty good one at the shorter distance.

I think Jordan was helped by watching and practicing threes with teammate Steve Kerr. Kerr, a Chicago Bulls guard who sometimes substituted for Jordan, made almost exactly half of his three-point attempts during the line-shortened three seasons.

Overall, for a 15-year career in which he substituted in 880 games and started only 30, Kerr's three-point percentage was .454. For the twelve seasons that were not marred by the shooting distance adjustment, his percentage was almost identical to Curry's.

If there was one aspect of basketball at which Steve Kerr was unexcelled it was three-point shooting.

LONG-RANGE ACCURACY

In this observer's opinion, Curry and Kerr were no better than equal in accuracy from long range to Pete Maravich. Unfortunately for Maravich, the three-point shot existed in the NBA only for his worn-out final season.

I saw televised games in which Maravich almost single-handedly beat and/or challenged to the finish nationally-ranked University of Kentucky teams for three years. He was, as we saw in chapter two, a TENDEX All-Time First Team college player.

In most cases, including Jordan's, the three-point adjustment for the three distance-shortened seasons has little impact on the overall rating. In Jordan's case he remains among the top four players of all-time, far above all the rest.

Of the other players rated according to the Shootist formula, Larry Bird came closest to 1.000 with a rating of .9994. With McHale, Ainge and Bird starting during the 1980s along with a fourth good shooter, Robert Parish, evidence favors that team's starting line-up as the best shooting unit of all-time.

One thing that amused me about those Celtics is the number of times their worst shooter, Dennis Johnson (FG% .445), took the key shots at the end of close games. This, of course, was long after the Celtics' front-office genius, Red Auerbach, had retired from the stressful head coaching job.

But, having been in close touch for many years with a man who knew Auerbach well, I think that Red probably shook his head in dismay every time the mediocre-shooting Johnson took and missed one of those shots.

A Celtics coach with a brain akin to Auerbach's would have tried to set up one of the four excellent shooters to take the shot, with an outlet-pass recipient (one of the other three) ready to catch and shoot in case the defense closed in on the designated shooter.

The fact that Johnson took so many of those shots indicates that the Celtics did not come up with good plans during late-game time-outs. The opponents, of course, calculated how they could force Johnson to receive the ball and take the big shots. The Celtics did not effectively counter the defensive plans.

Johnson about equaled his career field goal percentage of .445 on those shots. He got into the NBA Hall of Fame, for one thing, because he was so often the Celtics representative in post-game TV interviews after making (or missing) them.

And then there were the comments by Bird that Johnson was his greatest teammate, i.e., the team's best player other than himself. The explanation for that comment by Bird was simple: Most of the time when Johnson – officially but not actually the team's ball-controlling point guard – had the ball he looked for a chance to pass it to Bird, the point forward.

Bird ran the offense and his verbal praise let Johnson know he appreciated getting the ball from him.

McHale, Parish and Ainge could be counted on making at least half of their shots, so they were not reluctant about taking them. Often, when Bird threw a pass to one of these three, he did not get the ball back even when he called for it.

This was the best-shooting team I ever saw, with one noteworthy exception who somehow always seemed to take the most important shots.

UNJUST CRITICISMS

An interesting number is the Shootist stat for James Harden, .988. This would be among the top 20 on the overall list, if we listed them that far down. It is better than the numbers for excellent shooters including LeBron James .984, Jordan .963, Oscar Robertson .927, Pete Maravich .909 and Jerry West .905.

I have heard comments, and I don't think they are valid, criticizing the performance of Harden during the 2021 playoffs. He did shoot poorly, but…

…Having seen the Miami Heat's all-time greatest player, Dwyane Wade, lose his edge during the playoffs, once because of illness and another time because of an injury, I suspect that Harden's problem had to do with an injury that bothered him for half of the season. I do not think he choked.

I've also heard criticism of playoff performances of Robertson (from someone who never saw him during his prime). I know Robertson was not a choker, though he did tire toward the end of some seasons because of carrying the heaviest playing-time load of any backcourt player in NBA history. If there was any doubt, his superb play at both ends of the floor during his only chance to play in a Championship Series in 1970-71 was decisive.

So if you hear NBA fans talking down Robertson's or Harden's playoff performances, you have a choice: Don't listen to them...or tell them off.

THE VICINITY OF 1.000

We have estimated that a valid TENDEX rating for Robertson during that championship series, counting all valid assists, was about .900. Adding omitted assists to his record season after season would have moved his TENDEX rating to the vicinity of 1.000 numerous times. Russell Westbrook was not alone among point guards in that territory.

The best way to rate a player's value to his team is to look at the way the team plays after his departure. Harden six times in eight seasons with Houston registered the best TENDEX value rating in the NBA. This is the same statistic that rates Robertson, Jordan, Wilt Chamberlain and LeBron James at about the same level, nearly 20% higher than anyone else.

It's the most refined statistic in the TENDEX two-dozen. Let's talk about it briefly before concluding this commentary.

Value rating starts with the addition of a player's points, rebounds, assists, steals and blocked shots; next, the subtraction of all turnovers and missed shots; finally, three divisions.

The first two divisions for each player are carefully computed numbers representing team game pace (ball possessions) and a standard that involves the average ratings of all players in the league at the same position as the player being rated. Finally, a division for minutes played (durability).

Omission of a single factor can make a huge difference in the ratings. For example, it was the failure to include the standard rating for shooting guards while doing computations for Michael Jordan that cost Jordan, according to the errant 2003 *Total Basketball Encyclopedia*, all eight NBA Player of the Year awards that the TENDEX value rating statistic shows he deserved. The encyclopedia did not cite him as the league's best player for a single season.

Yes, I know, that's weird, but true, especially since the encyclopedia's editor, whom I met, was at that time a huge Jordan fan. I am surprised that he allowed that database to be printed.

At no time during James Harden's eight years with the team did Houston win an NBA title. But the Rockets were competitive in the playoffs. In fact, Harden helped his team make the playoffs in every one of those eight seasons and also in the other four seasons when Houston was not his team. Four times Harden's team has reached the NBA semi-finals, but never the Championship Series.

Three times, Harden has shot over .600 from two-point range in the playoffs with a high of .683, although that has been balanced by what, for him, is poor shooting from three-point range. Overall, his play in playoffs has been about the same as its regular-season excellence.

Still talking about Harden, it is rare for a player to help his team make the playoffs 12 seasons in a row, and equally rare for a team, which had made the playoffs for eight straight years, to finish dead-last in the NBA after that player left the team.

During 2020-21, after Harden's departure only eight games into the season, Houston finished last in the league with 17 victories. No other team won fewer than 20 games.

There is little doubt that the versatile Harden is a very significant NBA player, best overall in the league during the six years his value rating was No. 1.

There is no way of telling how good he could have been in the years before that, because Oklahoma City's coaching staff decided not to start him in the same backcourt with Russell Westbrook during Harden's first three seasons.

This happened even though Harden and Westbrook both were able to play either backcourt position, and the youthful Harden, even as a substitute, proved capable of holding his own when he was matched up with Kobe Bryant. Bryant at that time was rated by TENDEX among the three best players in the league.

I believe the decision not to give backcourt starter's minutes to Harden, with Westbrook, while Kevin Durant was excelling at small forward, probably cost OKC one or two, maybe even three, league titles. And for six years Harden was better than either of the other two men, who played a lot more minutes for OKC than he did.

A FEW QUESTION-MARKS

Robertson, Maravich and West were standout shooters who might have made our Shootist list (points per shot) if the league rules were the same when they played as they became with addition of the three-point shot. You only have to make one-third of those to achieve a 1.000 rating.

Maravich and West no doubt could have done a lot better than that. Robertson did not shoot from long range during his career because there was no benefit. He was able to average 30-plus points and connect on half of his field goal attempts, so why gun up a long shot that counts the same as a layup?

There is little doubt in my mind that, if it had been beneficial, Robertson would have practiced and made a high percentage from three-point range. He was strong enough so that three-pointers would have been well within his range; he had great shooting touch.

Robertson prided himself on excellence in all aspects of play.

Maravich and West proved to me that they could have done the same by often shooting from long-range during games, and making an excellent percentage, even though there was no reward for doing so: no third point.

The three-point shot did not exist when Robertson and West played, but overlapped Maravich's career by a single season. He attempted 15 three-pointers in his final year.

The Boston Celtics, ever alert for opportunities, had signed Maravich for that season perhaps because someone in the organization, probably Auerbach, recognized his extraordinary shooting range as a possible option for the Celtics when they needed a three-point field goal late in a game.

I'm not saying Maravich would have been a better three-point shooter by percentage than Curry. But Pete, I think, would have been a 1.000+ Shootist if he had three-point opportunities. He shot and made 25-footers throughout his varsity collegiate career at LSU when he was leading the NCAA in scoring consistently with an average of more than 40 points per game.

And, oh yes, about those 15 three-point attempts for the Celtics: The aging Maravich attempted those threes in 1978-79, mostly under late-game pressure.

He made two-thirds of them.

CHAPTER FIVE

PAR FOR THE PLAYMAKERS

Shooting and scoring numbers represent the first aspect of what I think has been the most popular TENDEX statistic. PAR (Points-Assists-Rebounds) has strongly influenced official NBA statistical records.

Without it, we might not have what the NBA calls triple-doubles, which was preceded by PAR.

And then there are the copycat stats. I don't think we would have seen them either. The one developed by Larry Bird was actually pretty good. Having been, along with Magic Johnson, the NBA's most prominent PAR players of the 1980s, Bird took pride in his versatility.

During that decade, after PAR was publicized in *The Sporting News*, you started hearing about triple-doubles, including at least 10 points, 10 rebounds and 10 assists by a player in a game. Bird and Johnson behaved at times as if they were inventors of the concept.

But when NBA statistical researchers began to realize that, if assists had been computed 20 years earlier in the same way as they were during the 1980s, and if triple-doubles were prominently publicized back then, Oscar Robertson's versatility put him in a class by himself.

I think that with triple-doubles prominently publicized, an injury-free Big O could have made his way through at least one entire season with nothing but triple-double games.

I think that, if he had not been prevented from entering the NBA after high school, or no later than his college freshman year, he would have averaged at least 10 points, rebounds and assists per game for nine NBA seasons, instead of six, and his scoring average during that period of time would have been about 30 points per game.

Even without the opportunity for early entry into the NBA or the favorable official scoring that later players enjoyed, Robertson did in fact average at least 10 points, assists and rebounds per game collectively for his first six NBA seasons.

His rebounds-per-game average for those six years was actually between 9.95 and 9.96. But the NBA rounds off numbers to the first decimal place, meaning that Robertson's average in the official league scenario was 10.0 rebounds per game for those six years.

Neither Johnson nor Bird ever has put together a triple-double season. Robertson is the career record holder in that department, even though it is a statistic that he probably heard little discussion about while he was playing.

Westbrook has averaged a triple-double for his last five NBA seasons, and in four of the five has averaged at least 10 points, rebounds and assists per game. He has officially broken two of Robertson's records.

But would he have that opportunity if there were not so many more assists available today than during the era when Robertson was playing? Several times Westbrook's assists average per game has been so slightly about 10.0 that it is doubtful that he could have stayed in double figures without those extra assists.

I can't help wondering if Robertson, had he concentrated on it, could have had at least one season early in his career when he averaged at least 15 assists and 15 rebounds per game along with his prime-career standard of 30 points.

Had he made it a goal, he might have done this in 1961-62, if his assists had been counted as they are under today's rules. He was a great athlete at that time, having averaged more than 15 rebounds per game for three NCAA seasons when the games were only 40 minutes long instead of 48.

His stats from early years when his athleticism was off the charts indicate that such an NBA season would have been possible for him at that time.

WE'RE UP TO PAR

Now let's talk some more about assists.

I am not going to make outrageous claims for Robertson regarding assists because the stats do not support them. His bulk PAR stats were unequaled because he played more minutes than any other guard in the game's history. For six consecutive years he averaged about 3,500 minutes per season.

Michael Jordan played a lot of minutes, too, but only once did Jordan total more than 3,300 minutes for a full season. The three men who held NBA career records for assists for the longest time were Robertson (about 20 years), Johnson (about 10) and John Stockton (the last 20).

Stockton's playmaking efficiency numbers are the best of the three men. By this I mean that, in consideration of team game-pace (the number of ball possessions), Stockton's assists totals were the best in the NBA. He is No. 1 in this category by a surprisingly big margin. He was the best playmaker of all-time.

Stockton made the greatest assist I ever saw. It was so good I think I mentioned it briefly in the NBA history chapter at the beginning of this book.

It was in the 1992 Olympic Games. A loose ball was bouncing out of bounds into a row of seats next to the court. Stockton made a lunge that turned into a horizontal leap after which he landed with a crash among the court-side seats.

When it became clear to an onlooker, Stockton's Utah Jazz teammate Karl Malone, that Stockton had a chance to get his hand on the ball before it landed out of bounds, Malone began running toward his offensive basket.

Stockton got his fingers on the ball with his right hand and somehow managed to do more than just knock it back inbounds. He slid his hand under the ball and launched it through the air behind his back.

It landed in the outstretched hands of Malone 25 feet away for what was an easy basket for Karl and an extraordinary assist for Stockton.

I also remember seeing Stockton's Utah team dominate Charles Barkley's team (I think it was Phoenix) in an NBA semi-finals series. Barkley became so frustrated by Stockton's extraordinary play that he knocked him down.

No whistle.

Barkley knocked Stockton down again, harder this time.

No whistle.

One more knockdown, a very hard one.

Finally, there was a personal foul call but no ejection of the popular Barkley, not even a warning.

Stockton, who showed no emotion during the entire painful sequence, sank both free throws and followed that with five or six points in the closing minutes of the game, clinching victory for Utah and a place in the finals against the Chicago Bulls.

The Jazz, by the way, gave the Bulls their toughest time during the six-championship sequence of the 1990s. It took several dubious and, in three cases, blatantly erroneous officiating calls to clinch things for the big-market team over the mini-mart team led by Stockton.

Too bad: The Jazz deserved that one. And a single championship-series defeat would in no way have marred the Bulls' dynastic accomplishments.

I think Stockton was one of the most underrated players in NBA history. In 1984, the year he was drafted, NBA scouts had him tentatively placed in the middle of the first round. Not having seen him – he played for a Gonzaga team which at that time did not have enough prominence to be nationally televised – I was surprised when his TENDEX rating put him in a flat tie with Barkley as the Nos. 3-4 players in the draft. Jordan was No. 1 and Hakeem Olajuwon No. 2.

TENDEX was exactly right in that draft. NBA scouts erred by dumping Jordan to No. 3 and Stockton all the way to No. 16. They also missed by a lot with their No. 2 selection behind Olajuwon, Sam Bowie.

I couldn't remember his name, had to look it up. But I did remember that Bowie, as a collegian, always appeared to me to be overrated. Another reason his name slipped my mind was that his NBA career was always mediocre in comparison with Jordan, who was drafted behind him...well, you know that story.

Here are the greatest NBA playmakers, from the TENDEX perspective:

1. John Stockton.
2. Oscar Robertson.
3. Magic Johnson.
4. Chris Paul
5. Russell Westbrook

These five are in a class by themselves. Extending the list to 12 players makes it include six more point guards – Steve Nash, Jason Kidd, Kevin Johnson, Mark Jackson, Isiah Thomas and Len Wilkens – plus one man who has spent most of his playing time at shooting guard, James Harden.

Harden makes the bottom of this list because for the last seven seasons he has ranked among NBA leaders in assists. He led the league once.

SPEAKING OF CHRIS PAUL

Now a few words about Paul. Only a technicality in contract expiration date prevented the Miami Heat from dominating the NBA's most recent decade with as much authority as that done during the 1990's by the Chicago Bulls. This story really began during the 2008 Olympic Games when Paul became friends with LeBron James and Dwyane Wade.

In those Games the most publicized player, Kobe Bryant, disappeared. Yes, I know he was the one who carried the American flag at the end, but that was because he had been named team captain. He did not excel on the playing floor.

Stars of the dominant American team were Wade, James and Paul. Even though he was relegated to substitute level behind Bryant, playing only about 17 minutes per game compared to 23 for Bryant, Wade was the individual standout.

He led the team in scoring with an average of almost a point per minute, and his other stats were outstanding, too. His TENDEX rating was by far the best on the team, in comparison with positional standards. The shooting guard position is the toughest one for achieving a high rating.

Next behind Wade in performance during the 2008 Games were James and Paul. Perhaps the only thing that kept Paul (instead of Chris Bosh) from joining Wade and James on the 2010-11 Miami Heat team was contract expiration date. Paul could not sign because he was still under contract with another team.

If Paul, who got along well with James and Wade during those Olympics, had signed with that Miami team, the NBA would either have grieved for the next six or seven seasons, as the Heat won title after title, or would have conceded the team's greatness.

Maybe, both.

This team was despised in New York, because James declined to sign with the Knicks and chose the Heat instead. Anti-Miami partiality was evident in refereeing of the 2010-11 NBA Championship Finals, which Miami led anyway through the first three games despite an injury to James' shooting elbow. Dallas finally won after Wade joined James on the injury list, even though both continued to play (but with mediocrity) until the finish.

After the 2008 Olympics, James knew that the Knicks had no one comparable to Wade, only the one-dimensional scorer Carmelo Anthony who had not excelled in the same Games.

James wanted to win NBA titles.

The Heat wound up making a mistake by signing Bosh to a big contract after those Olympics. Despite the injuries to both James and Wade in their first League Championship Series as teammates, they stuck together and the team came back to win the next two titles. The Heat reached the championship round all four years James and Wade were together.

They might have stayed together longer and won four or five titles if they had waited for a chance to sign Paul instead of signing Chris Bosh.

I have mentioned the extraordinary value ratings of Robertson, Jordan, James and Chamberlain. What I have not stressed is the fact that both Wade and Paul had individual seasons comparable to the four superstars mid-career value ratings (+60% or higher). The only other players to have done that are Kevin Durant (twice) and Harden.

Paul might be a better-known point guard than Stephen Curry right now, if he could have adjusted his contract expiration date and signed with the James/ Wade Miami team. Paul's career TENDEX value rating is better than Curry's.

The hypothetical Miami team might, indeed, have built a dynasty comparable to the Bulls. The Heat would have been no worse than equal to the Bulls with a superb threesome of James, Wade and Paul in comparison with Jordan, Pippen and Rodman/Horace Grant. Miami had no sixth man comparable to Toni Kukoc, however.

Rating systems I am familiar with place Jordan and James side by side. TENDEX locates Wade and Paul higher than Pippen and Rodman, much better than Grant.

Six of those seven men are, or will be NBA Hall of Famers. All six are in the upper half of the TENDEX top 75.

CHAPTER SIX

THE SURPRISING REBOUNDERS

I don't think I will be alone in astonishment at the TENDEX choices as the best three rebounders of all-time: Dennis Rodman (No. 1) and Moses Malone with Wes Unseld in a virtual tie for second place.

What happened to Wilt Chamberlain and Bill Russell? Their rebounds per game averages were much higher than this trio. They seem to be misfits at the No. 4 and 5 positions among all-time NBA rebounding leaders. According to all bulk statistics, they should be ranked No. 1 and 2.

For a few years after Rodman's retirement in the year 2000, I bit my lip whenever the topic of great NBA rebounders forced me into a discussion, or, horror of horrors, writing a book chapter on the subject.

But here we go again.

I almost always respect the TENDEX results when it comes to rating players, but in the case of all-time NBA rebounders, I already had settled it in my head that either Chamberlain or Russell was the greatest. Or maybe it should have been declared a first-place tie between the two men.

Who else could there be? These two men are the only ones with career averages of more than 20 rebounds per game. Chamberlain's numbers were a tad higher than Russell's but so were his minutes played.

And yet, every time I computed the stats, based on an incontrovertible TENDEX formula, Dennis Rodman came out ahead of both.

Only one man in NBA history has pulled down more than 20% of the rebounds available during his time on the floor. The number for that man, Dennis Rodman, is about 23%. Malone and Unseld are next at about 20%. In fact, Malone's number is exactly 20.0%. Russell and Chamberlain are in 19% territory.

And this is by far the best way to rate rebounders.

You first determine through existing statistics how many missed shots per game are available to be rebounded on average in games played by the contending player. Next, break that down to a smaller number by computing the player's percentage of the total minutes played.

If the two teams total 90 rebounds for the game, and the individual player being evaluated gets 15 of them while playing 40 minutes, he is in the 20% category, at least for that game.

Chamberlain sometimes played the full 48 minutes. In those games, he could achieve the 20% level by grabbing 20 rebounds if there were 100 available. He could do the same by snaring 18 rebounds in a game in which the total available was 90.

One complicating factor is that the three highest-rated players played fewer minutes per game than Chamberlain and Russell, and so were able to reach the same rating level, or even higher, while pulling down fewer rebounds.

There should be, and always are, in NBA statistical records minimal numbers of games and minutes played required to qualify in the ratings. The relevant statistical formula then is applied to every qualifying player.

The full-career NBA totals for Chamberlain were 22.9 rebounds per regular-season game, Russell 22.5, Unseld 14.0, Rodman 13.1 and Malone 12.2.

Now, I ask you, how is it even possible that Rodman was the greatest rebounder of all-time? It gets back to minutes played per game, and one or two other factors shortly to be discussed.

By playing about 32 minutes per game, or two-thirds of the time, Rodman met the qualifications. But his potential for acquiring big numbers of rebounds was far less than that of Russell and Chamberlain, who averaged more than 42 minutes. Unseld averaged about 36 and Malone 34.

Chamberlain, in 47,859 career minutes played, pulled in 23,924 rebounds. That's an average of almost exactly one rebound for every two minutes. Or one-half rebound per minute.

Russell's tally was similar, but a little better. He snared 21,620 rebounds in 40,726 minutes, slightly more than one for every two minutes of playing time.

Rodman, who played during an era when hardly anybody averaged over 40 minutes per game, as Chamberlain and Russell had done, was a second-string player for much of his career. He played more than

3,000 minutes in only one season and wound up with 11,954 rebounds in 28,839 minutes.

His rebounding average per minute was .415, a substantial distance behind Russell and Chamberlain.

Rodman made up most of the difference based on game-pace. For instance, Russell's team, the Celtics, averaged between 115 and 120 points per game during most of his 13-year career. The scoring numbers of Chamberlain's teams during the same era were similar.

The game-pace of that era was very fast, meaning that there were a lot more ball possessions with potential for taking (and missing) more shots and piling up statistics in every aspect of play. including rebound opportunities..

Careful computations of game pace, especially total shots missed resulting in rebounds, shoved Rodman far enough ahead of the other two men that there is no point in trying to declare the results a tie, as I was inclined to do in the contest between Chamberlain and Russell.

This is because the decade in which Rodman excelled was the slowest-paced since the NBA's most ancient decade between 1946 and 1955. The greatest leap forward in that category took place during the late 1960's when Russell and Chamberlain were playing.

That's when players stopped walking and started running. The style for the earliest seasons of the league and for most of the 1990's was for the point guard to walk the ball up instead of throwing it to up to an open teammate who had a chance to take a good shot or to throw a pass to a teammate who did.

Oscar Robertson had a lot to do with the change.

He described the difference in a single sentence: "We passed the ball a lot more than they did."

Rodman played half of his career with a defense-minded Detroit team that was releasing a lot less shots and permitting a lot less than those of Russell's and Chamberlain's teams.

This game-pace factor erased the deficit for Rodman, but I was still surprised at the final outcome of the rebounding statistical ratings.

Sometimes you just have to believe the arithmetic: During games played by these three men, Malone, Unseld and whoever else you want to include in the conversation, Rodman was the only one who was able to haul in more than 20% of the total available rebounds during his minutes on the floor.

And he had a significant margin over the next four guys.

Here is a statistic of Rodman's that has to impress you, even if you are (like me) a doubter: It is that Dennis, in seasons that he led the NBA in rebounding, often had a winning margin of as many as three or four rebounds per game over the No. 2 man.

An important number for Rodman is this: He led the NBA in rebounds per game for seven straight seasons. Malone did it six times, but not consecutively. Russell was the league-leader in the same category five times. Chamberlain led a record 11 times, but played more minutes than the other leaders. Unseld led only once but was a model of consistency.

When all factors are considered, the numbers are close. A lot of Rodman's contemporaries played more minutes than he did. Chamberlain played enough more than Russell to gain the advantage most of the time in total rebounds even though Russell edged ahead of him in the most important category, rebounds per opportunities.

But here's the most surprising thing of all: The difference between .19 (Chamberlain's and Russell's bottom-line rebounding percentage) and .23 (Rodman's) is more than four per cent.

These numbers are not to be subtracted but divided. Rodman's statistical edge over Russell and Chamberlain in rebounding was close to 20%. He got about 20% more of the available rebounds than did the other two men.

Yes, it's hard to believe, but there it is.

I was about to conclude this chapter with the comment that TENDEX is usually right. But that isn't accurate: TENDEX almost *always* is right and the margin of difference in this case is large enough to be considered proof

No matter what you or I might be inclined to believe, Dennis Rodman was the greatest NBA rebounder of all-time.

CHAPTER SEVEN

DEFENSE: THE THREE R'S

Exactly half of the game of basketball involves defense. But there is little evidence other than final scores that defensive tactics and strategy are as important as offensive ones. They don't show a lot of outstanding defensive plays on the Sports Center highlights. Those are all about who scored the most points and made the most spectacular plays to score those points.

But it is an incontrovertible truth that the individual players on winning teams have as important defensive roles as offensive ones. To win a game, you must play better overall on a combination of offense and defense, than your opponent. It is possible to overcome a so-so offensive performance by having an exceptionally good defensive one.

Maybe you have had the opportunity to observe practice sessions of an NBA team. I have seen some of those. But I can't remember seeing very many in which the primary emphasis was holding position to block out opponents from breaking through for offensive rebounds leading to easy put-back baskets.

Usually the emphasis focuses on a few plays being injected into a game by a coach who thinks they will work against the defense anticipated to be played by the opponent.

Defensive plays, with the exception of blocked shots, are not nearly as visually impressive as offensive ones. Not as spectacular as a round-house slam dunk or a three-point shot released from below shoulder level that swishes net.

I know from experience that NBA players do not like to be told they have failed to box out an opponent. I remember one player so ignorant of the technique that when an opponent backed into him to gain rebounding position he became enraged.

During the ensuing play at the other end of the floor, the angry victim of the box-out was pouring out verbal expletives while his more skilled opponent was grinning all the way to the basket for two points.

The reason players do not like to be told they have failed to box out makes more sense than becoming enraged by an opponent who successfully boxes you out. This is because coaches do not like players to miss assignments. They have a tendency to force guilty players to practice and practice until they are able to do what they have been told.

This includes, at least occasionally, boxing out.

From my perspective, as the statistician designated by a coach to keep specific track of box-out failures, I have been forced to listen to loud contentions by culpable players. I have been told by a player that he actually had not missed his assignment, but that I had missed, or misinterpreted, the play.

At any rate, this chapter is about defense. No, I will not take into account whether you read it or not, as long as you go on and read the chapters after this one. I understand why you don't enjoy reading about boxing out and other defensive intangibles.

It's boring.

But it wins games.

TWO TYPES OF DEFENSE

Let's divide the rest of this chapter into two categories: Big-play defense and man-to-man.

The greatest big-play defender in NBA history, in my opinion, was Bill Russell. He made one great defensive play after another, after which, inspired teammates often took the ball to the other end of the court and scored.

The only defensive plays for which statistics are kept are blocked shots and steals. Neither of these stats was tallied when Russell and Wilt Chamberlain were playing.

According to my conversations with a statistician who kept track of the blocked shots and steals computations for many games involving Russell and/or Chamberlain, the two men both averaged between four and five blocked shots during their prime seasons.

My estimates for both men were about 4.5 per game, but I gave Russell a few more than Chamberlain because it seemed to me that when the smaller Russell blocked a shot, recovered the ball and passed it to a teammate that it more often resulted in a basket than when Chamberlain did the same thing.

Actually, I think Russell did it more often than Chamberlain.

Defense was what Russell did best, so I credited him the maximum for it, especially since he was the best player on the NBA's best team most of the time. Chamberlain (rarely) and Oscar Robertson (never in his prime decade) had teammates who could compete with Russell's.

And so I also was liberal with the numbers I assigned to Russell for steals. My recollection is that Russell was uncanny in his timing for jumping out from behind the man he was guarding to pick off an entry pass. His steals were legitimate.

Steals that I consider illegitimate are those made at the expense of man defense. Popular players including Allen Iverson, Jerry West and Dennis Johnson, all too often were beaten off the dribble and then tried to reach in from the side or even from behind for a steal attempt. Maybe twice a game they would get one, but not nearly as often as the opposing team scored baskets because of the man defense breakdown.

If one of these men led the NBA in steals, it was a stat to be ignored, not factored into the annual all-league defensive selections. Sadly, those men sometimes did receive a lot of all-league defensive team votes. The great man defenders, who did not have impressive steals or blocked-shots numbers, too often were ignored.

I'm not sure if Russell ever stole the ball 200 times in a season, as has been claimed by one old-timer. But there is no doubt in my mind that Russell was the greatest big-play defender in NBA history.

Chamberlain was a good defender, not a great one. He actually learned a lot by observing the more experienced Russell. Russell was about equal to Wilt as a rebounder, but there was no contest at the offensive end of the floor. When the final numbers were tallied for the two men, Chamberlain had averaged about 30 points per game for his entire career. Russell's average was about 15, not bad for a 35-minutes-per-game player but terrible for one who played 45.

Chamberlain's field-goal percentage was much better than Russell's. Russell was slightly better than Wilt from the free-throw line, but both men shot in the so-so range between .500 and .600.

Wilt, like his monstrous successor, Shaq O'Neal, was too strong to have much of a touch from the free-throw line, but both men had high field goal percentages because they got to the basket so effectively. Russell did very little effectively on offense. All-around shooting and scoring were among his deficiencies.

Chamberlain was the better overall player by a wide margin. But Russell was a better defender, especially when it came to big plays.

Rounding out the top-five on my big-play defensive list are shot-blockers Hakeem Olajuwon and David Robinson, plus Dennis Rodman, who made a variety of big plays to shut down high-scoring opponents, steal or rebound the ball under the noses of the most tenacious offensive players.

This overlaps into the other aspect of defensive play, in fact, the most important aspect: man-to-man defense. We have discussed how Oscar Robertson shut down opponent after opponent in All-Star Games and capped his career by victimizing Hall of Famer Earl (the Pearl) Monroe in the 1971 NBA Championship Series. Even though he had entered the twilight of his career, the Big O dominated that match-up at both ends of the court.

Robertson seemed to do that all the time to every star player he defended. His biggest victim, as I recall, was his 1960 Olympic backcourt teammate Jerry West, who became a perennial all-star NBA guard. Robertson also fared very well against Hall of Famers Dave Bing and John Havlicek, both of whom said praiseful things about him.

Strange the things you remember, but I recall having a big laugh over a play when Robertson trapped West in a corner of the court and was in process of forcing a turnover. All of a sudden, seemingly from nowhere, a rookie teammate of the Big O's jumped between Robertson and West.

Taking advantage of the screen being applied for him inadvertently, West jumped over the rookie, sank a long shot and grinned at the angry Robertson, who was telling the rookie off.

DEVASTATING DEFENSE

This shows two things about Robertson: His devastating defense (there was no way West was going to get that shot off if the rookie hadn't jumped in the way) and his intensity for the sport. I doubt if that rookie ever received a scolding, even from a head coach, equaling the one Robertson gave him.

Robertson was the best man-to-man defender I ever saw. No. 2 in that category was Rodman. And so, with high finishes in both aspects of defense, Dennis takes second place behind Russell and a tad ahead of Robertson for overall TENDEX defensive honors.

It is the only time when Robertson's name is mentioned prominently in this book without him being declared No. 1 in the topic of discussion. Robertson was No. 3 this time. But when you combine that with his overall No. 1 standing on offense, he's (at this moment, at least) the strongest contender to wind up as the overall No. 1in the final chapter of this book.

No, don't go there now. We haven't finished yet with defense.

Russell was not among the top three man-to-man defenders. Nor was Robertson at that level among the big-play defenders. The clearest example I ever saw of Rodman's dominant defense was the way, game after game, he humiliated official NBA Hall of Famer James Worthy. I never saw Worthy have a good game against Rodman's defense.

In one game, Rodman drew an offensive foul from Worthy and landed on the seat of his pants. He then limped off the floor for treatment of a bruised tailbone while Worthy ran wild, scoring basket after basket.

The announcer for the game, whose identity I mercifully do not remember, spent nearly all of the remainder of that game talking about how great was the defense being played against Worthy by Rodman's replacement.

I remember him saying at least once that the pathetic substitute was a better defender than Rodman.

The only thing worse than the substitute's defense was the analysis of it by the announcer. Worthy was a good offensive player, to be sure, but not nearly as good as Rodman's substitute made him appear to be. Neither was he as bad as Rodman made him look in game after game.

The reason I give an edge to Robertson over Rodman in man defense is that in big games I never saw the man assigned to Robertson for primary coverage have what could be called an excellent performance.

Rodman wasn't as good against everybody as he was against Worthy, whose moves to the basket were at least a step slower than Dennis' reaction time. But there were players in the league, Larry Bird, Michael Jordan and a few others, who could beat Rodman some of the time.

Worthy seemed helpless against Rodman who, all things considered, from my perspective, was the second-best individual defensive player in NBA history.

Russell edged Rodman and Robertson for No. 1 because of the difference in big-play defense. Rodman and Robertson might have been better than Russell in man defense, but Russell was in a class by himself with his big plays at the defensive end of the floor.

These were the all-time TENDEX leaders in the three categories discussed in this chapter:

Overall Best Defenders:
1. Bill Russell.
2. Dennis Rodman.

3. Oscar Robertson
4. Hakeem Olajuwon.
5. Michael Cooper.

Best Big-Play Defenders:
1. Russell.
2. Olajuwon.
3. Wilt Chamberlain,
4. David Robinson.
5. Rodman

Best Man-to-Man Defenders
1. Robertson.
2. Rodman.
3. Cooper
4. Sidney Moncrief,
5. Russell.

As a final point in this chapter, I think it is good to interject here that LeBron James and Michael Jordan both would have earned Second Team honors (between No. 6 and No. 10) in one of the two defensive categories we have discussed. They were very good defensive players.

It has been established that, according to the most accurate of the two-dozen TENDEX formulae, the foursome of Robertson-Chamberlain-James-Jordan are far ahead of every other player on any valid all-time list for overall play. The fact that all four have been good-to-excellent defenders doesn't improve the chances of anyone else being mentioned in the same breath with them in final comparisons.

CHAPTER EIGHT

UNDERRATED AND OVERRATED

The overall atmosphere sought to be projected in this book is one of positivity – highlights, not lowlights of NBA history. And so in the previous chapter much more emphasis was placed on strong defensive players than weak ones. In this chapter more will be said about underrated players than overrated ones. We shall leave the overrated category for brief consideration at the end.

As a basketball fan, I find it interesting and challenging to identify players who excel in important aspects of play but receive little credit for it because they don't talk a lot about themselves, or they play in small markets, or for lousy teams, or maybe their style of play is unconventional,

Following are the 10 NBA players I have identified as the most underrated during the league's 75 seasons. Each reader could probably add a few names to the list. It ranges from excellent players who have received too little acclaim to players with average talent who have exceeded their apparent potential.

THE UNDERRATED

I decided not to list these in order because I was having a tough time deciding in what order to list them.

The categories explored in this book are so broad as to entail everything good and/or bad about a player. TENDEX can tell you a lot, but hasn't produced a statistical formula for relating the intangibles of personality and popularity. Underrated implies lack of the kind of adulation and popularity that a player's outstanding performance level would normally deserve.

The 10 selected, in no particular order, are Michael Cooper, Richie Guerin, Pete Maravich, Moses Malone, John Havlicek, Dominique Wilkins, Rick Barry, James Harden, Dwyane Wade, and Oscar Robertson.

These players range all the way from superstardom (Robertson) to present anonymity (Cooper and Guerin). More than half of them achieved stardom in the league, but none, in my opinion, received the noisy applause their performances cried out for.

I suspect that my mention of Cooper in this book's chapter on defense may have been the first time many readers saw this guy's name in print. So let's start with him.

1. **Michael Cooper**: No. 3 on the man defense list behind Robertson and Rodman, but how much more mention have these other two received than Cooper in this book and everywhere else, even though both have been somewhat underrated themselves? This fact alone is legitimate cause to rank Cooper at or near the top of the NBA's most underrated list. But there is more. The Los Angeles Lakers could not have won five of their titles during

the 1980s without Cooper. It's possible they might not have won any of them. Even though Cooper did not start during that decade, he always played between half and two-thirds of the team minutes. He was, in fact, the sixth man, though his role was different from most sixth men, who are predominantly scorers. Cooper was one of the best man defenders in the NBA and his assignment was usually to substitute for a player, Magic Johnson, whose lone deficiency on a basketball court was man defense. And so, with the popular Johnson and the unheralded Cooper playing team-leading roles at opposite ends of the court, the Lakers won all those titles.

2. **Pete Maravich**: The American Basketball Association (ABA) changed the game. Biggest change was introduction of a three-point shot from a distance (25 feet) that, through careful experimentation, the league decided was fair because the players made about 30% of their shots from there. This, in the scoring column, is equivalent to the norm of 45% from two-point range. It is mentioned re Maravich because he is the only player (including Steph Curry) whom I am convinced could have made 45% from the 25-foot distance for his full career. Saw Maravich actually do that in many televised games of the LSU team he played for. Maravich was such a great college player that

he made the TENDEX NCAA First-Team of all-time. He often scored 50 points in college games, nearly always at least 40. Many came on shots that were released about 25 feet from the basket. If he were playing college ball today, with its shorter three-point shot, he'd likely be averaging 50 points per game.

3. **Richie Guerin**: During the season (1961-62) when I became statistician for the New York Knicks, Guerin ranked among the league leaders with his scoring average of 29.5 points per game. But, despite his star quality and the fact that he played in the biggest market of them all, he got virtually no notice from anyone about anything, other than TENDEX, which gave him by far the best rating of the Knicks players of that era. Like Wilt Chamberlain, Guerin spent quite a bit of time checking out his TENDEX rating. He was rarely disappointed.

4. **John Havlicek**: With the help of glib coach Red Auerbach, Bill Russell was honored as the greatest player of the NBA's first 50 years. No mention was made of Havlicek, although a sound argument could be made that Havlicek was as great a player as Russell. Russell's deficiency was offense. After Havlicek learned to hit shots from 20-foot range, there were no serious defects in his game. He was the Celtics' best offensive player and second-best defensive player of the Red Auerbach era. It is argued

that Russell proved he was the greatest NBA player by winning the most league titles (11). Havlicek won "only" eight, but two of them came after all of the other great players of the Celtic dynasty retired. Havlicek's final two titles came with teammates far inferior to the ones Russell had for all 13 seasons of his career. Counting league titles alone, the top four players in NBA history were: Russell 11, Sam Jones 10, Havlicek 8, K.C. Jones 8. Are we to believe the four Celtic teammates all – or any of the four – were greater than Jordan, Chamberlain, Robertson and James? Titles are important, but teammates are more important. No teammates, no titles.

5. **Moses Malone**. A friend, former standout NBA coach Del Harris, has told me that Malone was his favorite player. Harris, who coached Malone during his six peak seasons in Houston, said this about him: "He got out on the playing floor early and stayed late. He never took a play off." Moses already has been mentioned in this book as one of the top three rebounders in league history. He won three MVP awards. Led Philadelphia to a league championship in 1983 and was chosen over Julius Erving as MVP of the Championship Series. Combining 19 NBA seasons with two in the ABA, he built a record-setting professional basketball career of 21 seasons, one

season longer than legendary Kareem Abdul-Jabbar. I chose him for this list because I cannot remember reading a feature article about him in any publication. I'm sure some good things were written about him, but in comparison with his deserving performance, not nearly enough of them. Maybe it was coincidental, but to me it seemed strange that so great a player could receive so little recognition.

6. **Dominique Wilkins**: Spectacular athlete with leaping ability generating enough time for him to complete more different kinds of slam dunks than any other player I ever saw, including Michael Jordan. Led the NBA in scoring once, and averaged about 25 points per game for a full 15-season career. Was selected behind No. 1 James Worthy and No. 2 Terry Cummings in the 1982 NBA draft. TENDEX ranked those three players in the reverse order of their selection and, as usual, proved correct. Wilkins couldn't even catch an even break in a slam-dunk contest, "losing" one year to Michael Jordan in a scenario so strongly biased for Jordan that it was laughable. The NBA's TV announcers often tended to underrate Wilkins' great play in televised games I saw.

7. **Rick Barry**: Barry was as athletic and as fundamentally sound a player as almost anybody. But it was his ability to pile up points in a hurry that set him apart. TV announcers

would joke that he never saw a shot he didn't like. But this was true of Allen Iverson, not Rick Barry. Barry actually ranked among the top three or four playmaking small forwards of all-time, after LeBron James and Larry Bird. His ball-handling and passing were excellent and his free-throw shooting has been bettered only by that of Steph Curry. After sustaining a severe knee injury while playing in the ABA, he bounced back to lead Golden State to an "upset" NBA title in 1974-75. He averaged 30 points per game that season and was the Championship Finals MVP. After that unexpected victory by the Warriors, Barry was praised good-naturedly by a black teammate who said about him with a smile and tongue in cheek: "For a white boy, he's pretty good."

8. **James Harden**: With the exception of one major disappointment – the 2021 playoffs – this man has been nothing but outstanding. And yet, the negative comments I have heard about him have been more than the positives. I heard muttering about him choking while the Brooklyn Nets were losing to the Milwaukee Bucks in the '21 playoffs. But the only thing he really did wrong was to get injured and try to play while he was subpar physically. He played nine of the 12 games in those playoffs for the Nets, but was hampered by injury all the way. I did not hear a word of praise for

him winning six TENDEX Player of the Year honors and five win-shares titles. He ranked in both categories as the player of the decade for 2011-2020. Win-shares, in my opinion, is the best non-TENDEX statistic. Its similar results to TENDEX value ratings from year to year may have influenced my thinking a bit.

9. **Dwyane Wade**: After picking Wade with the No. 5 choice in the 2003 draft, Miami for the first time became a force in the NBA, winning three titles and reaching the playoff finals five times during his tenure with the team. None of this could have been accomplished without Wade because it was his friendship and mutual respect with LeBron James that led to James joining the team before the 2010-11 season. With James hindered by a shooting elbow injury, Wade was on his way to leading Miami to a second championship victory over Dallas in 2011, averaging over 31 points per game for three games before suffering a hip-pointer injury. After the injury, Miami lost three in a row. His amazing block of a Kevin Durant three-point attempt in the 2012 Championship Series, won by Miami, was the best I ever saw. The officials ruled it goal-tending, but when Wade caught the ball at the free-throw line, intelligent observers knew it was scientifically impossible that the ball had been on its way down while traveling only one-third of the

way to the rim. He holds the NBA record for most blocked shots by a shooting guard. He almost-single-handedly led the Heat to victory over Dallas in the 2006 Championship Series in what may have been the greatest four consecutive games ever played in the playoffs, Wade averaged over 39 points per game as the Heat won all four after having lost two straight by double-figure margins when he was ill, but tried to play anyway. The NBA scoring record for a full Championship Finals series is over 37 points per game.

10. **Oscar Robertson**: There is so much in this book about Robertson that it might almost be called his biography, so let's keep this short. In order to make sure Robertson belongs on this list let's do one thing: Let's ask 10 NBA fans, who have not read this book, each to list their choices as the top 10 players of all-time. My prediction: Not one of these lists will contain the name of Robertson. And, even if he is on a list, his name will be near the bottom. He is one of the top four players of all-time, arguably No. 1. But nearly all NBA fans I have known have been unaware of the greatness of Robertson. They have heard great things about Wilt Chamberlain and Bill Russell, but not Robertson, who was better than Russell by a significant margin and at least as good as Chamberlain.

Now for the most overrated, and I'm sure to get a lot of NBA fans angry at me for this. But here goes: Based on analyses made so far in this book, one name that obviously should be on this list is Bill Russell. It isn't that he was not a great player, but he was not *the greatest* of all-time as the voting turned out during the league's 25th and 50th anniversary celebrations. He was the greatest big-play defender in league history, but was so weak offensively that Red Auerbach often "rested" him by allowing him to remain in backcourt while the other four players moved the ball into offensive position. The Celtics seemed to score just as many points in those situations as they would have if Russell had played offense with the other four. His awesome defense makes him the No. 20 player overall of all-time (see chart at the end of book). But not No.1.

Another popular player who belongs among the overrated, but is named only with reluctance, is Magic Johnson. Without the presence of Cooper to play most of the backcourt defense with Byron Scott, Magic's weak defense would have offset much of his great offense and could have been costly to the Lakers in their drive for five NBA titles. He was adequate in the back row of the illegal two-three zone the Lakers played at that time.

Next on our all-overrated list is Johnson's All-Star Game playmate Isiah Thomas. He and Johnson looked great playing against the pathetic defense they offered each other. Thomas' TENDEX rating actually was a few points higher than Johnson's for their cumulative match-up in eight All-Star games. It was more than 200 percentage points higher than Thomas' normal rating (against better defense). Johnson had a much higher rating than Thomas when the two weren't playing head-to-head and the Lakers were in their usual zone defense.

Completing the top ten overrated players, in no particular order: Dennis Johnson, Allen Iverson, Bill Bradley, Joe Fulks, Joe Dumars, James Worthy, Bob Cousy.

CHAPTER NINE

DURABILITY AND TENACITY

The most durable players are those who play the most minutes at the highest level. Let's take for example a comparison between Oscar Robertson and Russell Westbrook, two of the best all-around guards in NBA history.

In one of his triple-double seasons, 2016-17, Westbrook maintained a TENDEX rating of 1.000 for the entire season, highest rating ever achieved by an NBA guard. However, his value rating was only +61.7% above the norm for the point guard position. This number was the highest in the league that season, but over the course of NBA history has been topped many times by other players.

The all-time best was Robertson's +89.1% in 1963-64. And yet, Robertson's best pure TENDEX rating for a full season was .891 in 1961-62, more than 100 percentage points below Westbrook's best. How is this possible?

It has to do mostly with minutes played. In a normal season during his prime, Robertson played about 3,500 minutes. That wore him down so that he fatigued late in games and, especially, late in his career. Leg injuries bothered him, especially toward the end. If he had played normal minutes, I believe he could have had several 1.000 seasons in which fatigue did not play a major role.

He did surpass 1.000 three times in college when his legs were still strong. It is noteworthy here that college ratings on average are only about 80% as high as NBA ratings.

Robertson's fatiguing NBA minutes came about because his coaches couldn't help noticing the difference in performance by the Cincinnati team when he was not on the floor. The Royals, who won 55% of their games when Robertson was healthy throughout his career, could not seem to win at all without him.

And so his coaches wore him out so that they would not have to endure, in his place on the floor, substitutes whose performance would be less than half as productive as his.

This is a good place, I think, for mentioning a statistic about Robertson that embarrasses his critics. I heard it said by one of them that Naismith Hall of Famer Nate (Tiny) Archibald was a better player than Robertson. The Cincinnati Royals acquired Archibald to replace Robertson at point guard when the Big O signed with Milwaukee after 10 years in Cincinnati.

The Royals won 40% of their games during the first Archibald season, 15% less than they had won with Robertson. Moreover, in 1959-60, the season before acquiring Robertson, Cincinnati won only about 25% of its games.

So for the 10 Robertson seasons, the ratio of team victories with Robertson in comparison with victories in the seasons immediately before and after, without him, was 55% to 33%. That 5-to-3 victory ratio is one of the most impressive stats I have seen demonstrating a player's value to his NBA team.

WESTBROOK'S ACCOMPLISHMENTS

For Westbrook, the norm has been about 2,500 minutes per season. He did play about 2,800 in his MVP season (2016-17) and he had Robertson-like statistics with over 30 points, 10 rebounds and 10 assists per game. On the negative side were 438 turnovers (more than five per game) and a field-goal shooting percentage of .425. Robertson normally hit about half of his field goal attempts.

But there was no disputing the TENDEX rating, best ever for an NBA guard.

The difference is that for every 3,500-minute season Robertson had, Westbrook has had one of about 2,500 minutes played, one-thousand less than Robertson.

Those minutes must be played by substitutes and the average No. 2 NBA point guard maintains a TENDEX rating of about .400. That is, 600 percentage points below Westbrook's best and nearly 500 below Robertson's.

Now, we know why the coaches overworked Robertson. In the end, it takes its toll by shortening the player's career, unless, like Michael Jordan, he quits and takes a rest for a couple of seasons.

Jordan may be criticized for doing what he did. Maybe during his first so-called retirement lasting nearly two full seasons, he did cost the Bulls an NBA championships. He did play in the playoffs at the end of the second retirement season, but he wasn't near his normal performance level and the team lacked its usual cohesion.

On the other hand, if he was really as fatigued as I believe he must have been after leading the team to three straight league titles during pressure-packed playoff situations, maybe he did the team a favor by restoring his leg strength during those two seasons. He did play baseball, but that sport does not put nearly as much pressure on the legs as does basketball.

Later, after three more titles, Jordan "retired" again, this time for three years. Despite advancing age for a basketball player (mid-30's), his play during those last three title seasons (after nearly two full years of rest) was, surprisingly, almost as good as the first three.

So this is not a criticism of Jordan (for recognizing his need of rest), nor of a coach's decision to keep Westbrook's minutes played at a level the coach recognized as comfortable for the player. It is simply a way of explaining why Robertson, with a best full-season TENDEX rating below .900 can be said to be a superior player to Westbrook, whose rating went as high as 1.000.

On the distinctly positive side in rating Jordan's level of durability, he four times led the NBA in games played for a full season and twice in minutes played.

Overall, for full career, Robertson's basic TENDEX rating is better than Westbrook's. But Robertson's superior defensive play and durability assert him at a much higher overall level. This is validated by his TENDEX value rating.

Despite his extraordinary versatility, in overall career performance rated by TENDEX, Westbrook trails not only Robertson, but also, among contemporary guards, Chris Paul and James Harden. It's a close call between Westbrook and Steph Curry, but both men trail Robertson, Paul, Harden, John Stockton and Magic Johnson.

Robertson played through the kind of grind that has resulted in the shortening of careers of other players who tried to play even as many as 3,000 minutes per season, let alone 3,500. Robertson was an amazingly durable player, as was Wilt Chamberlain, who holds nearly all of the NBA's minutes-played records.

Bill Russell, too, played a lot of minutes, but we have mentioned the breaks he took while "resting" at the defensive end of the floor during game action. His durability is not to be compared with the other two but he ranks not far behind them in this category in comparison with other NBA players.

Chamberlain was able to play more minutes than Robertson primarily because his position (center) was not nearly as demanding on the legs as was Robertson's (point guard).

When it came to the double-D's – defense and durability – Russell was the absolute best at the first but not the second. Robertson was No. 1 in both categories among point guards and very close to No. 1 including everybody else.

We are not going to select the least durable players in this chapter, but let's fill out a 10-player roster of durability on the positive side after the most durable center in NBA history, in terms of minutes played per season, Chamberlain; and the most durable guard, Robertson.

1. Wilt Chamberlain.
2. Oscar Robertson.
3. Karl Malone.
4. Kareem Abdul-Jabbar
5. LeBron James
6. Michael Jordan
7. Allen Iverson
8. Bill Russell
9. Elvin Hayes
10. Moses Malone

Isn't it interesting that the top four players of all-time in the NBA, according to TENDEX value ratings, all have places among the top six on the durability list above?

Chamberlain nearly always accomplished what he set out to do. In the 1961-62 season, after deciding he wanted to play every minute of every game, he came within one game of achieving that goal while averaging 48.5 minutes per game.

That same season, Chamberlain set a league record with his average of 50.4 points per game. It was the only season in which an NBA player averaged more than a point per minute. The next closest was James Harden with an average of 36.1 points in 36.8 minutes in the 2018-19 season.

The only other season in which an NBA player has averaged more than 40 points per game for a full season was 1962-63 when Wilt's average was 44.8.

Wilt also was one-two in the record book in two categories involving minutes played. He holds the NBA record with five consecutive seasons leading in total minutes played and also is in a second-place tie with Jordan, each with three. Wilt's total of eight was No. 1 by a wide margin.

Also, as might be suspected, Wilt has a similar advantage in consecutive seasons leading the league in minutes per game. Wilt had a five-season streak followed a year later by a four-season streak. Except for injury in the interim year, Wilt might have done it 10 times in a row.

Chamberlain's competition at that time, Russell and Robertson, ended up in second and third place respectively behind Wilt in career minutes per game. Wilt's record mark in that category is 45.8 – more than three minutes better than Russell (42.3) and Robertson (42.2).

The names changed in career minutes played because Moses Malone (21), Kareem Abdul-Jabbar (20), and Karl Malone (19) played more seasons than Chamberlain (14), Robertson (14) and Russell (13).

Kareem's career minutes totaled an NBA record 57,446 and Karl Malone was second with 54,852. Moses Malone totaled 49,444. But on seasonal average these three were not close to Chamberlain, Russell and Robertson.

LeBron James, whose career has featured three seasons in which he led the NBA in minutes played, is closing in on Karl Malone and Abdul-Jabbar. With a total of of 50,055 minutes played in 18 seasons, James has a chance to catch Karl Malone with two more solid seasons and Abdul-Jabbar with three. He is not as yet showing serious signs of slowing down.

This was Kareem's only durability record that I could find. He never led the NBA in minutes for a full season, which is ironic in that he led all players with his career total.

Moses Malone led the NBA twice in minutes for a full season. Karl Malone had a remarkable record of playing in at least 80 regular-season games during 17 of his 19 NBA seasons.

THE UNFAVORITE

A careful reader of this book knows by now that Allen Iverson was not among the author's favorite players. But to Iverson's credit, his record of minutes played demonstrates genuine durability.

Seven times Iverson led the NBA in minutes played for full seasons, two short of Chamberlain's record. Iverson had two streaks of three seasons in a row leading the league in that category.

Chamberlain set the rookie record for minutes per game during the 1959-60 season with 46.4. Elvin Hayes edged out Wilt for total minutes played by a rookie with 3,695 in 1968-69.

One other record is worthy of mention. In a multiple-overtime game on Nov. 9, 1989, Dale Ellis

(69) and Xavier McDaniel (68) entered the record book in the category of most minutes played in a single game.

To me, however, the most impressive category is minutes per game for a full career. Despite late-career diminishment, the records of Chamberlain playing 45.8 minutes per career game, without any kind of rest and Robertson playing 42.2 minutes per career game, much of it involving intense man defense against all-star caliber guards, were amazing numbers.

CHAPTER TEN

VERSATILITY AND ATHLETICISM

Important themes of this chapter are the most versatile and outstanding athletes ever to play in the NBA.

There are some surprises, including one player who did not actually play NBA basketball, but obviously could have played if he hadn't placed the sports of football and baseball higher on his priority list.

I doubt if you can guess who will head the list of ten players featured on the next few pages.

I knew this man was an outstanding athlete, but until doing the research would not have picked him as the most versatile athlete ever to play in the NBA. Versatility here is being defined as the number of major sports, in addition to basketball, in which an athlete excels.

Two players are included who, as far as I know, excelled in no sport other than basketball. But their athleticism on the basketball floor was so extraordinary that I decided to work them into the mix. With their court-coverage potential, I think they could have been excellent tennis players if they had seriously taken up that sport.

The No. 1 player on this list did play a lot of tennis. He was so good at it that, even though he played only during the basketball off-season, he was capable of walking into the clubhouse of just about any tennis club in the U.S.A., challenging the resident head pro to a match and, most of the time, defeating him.

His brother, Dennis, told me he did this on a regular basis.

His name is Rick Barry.

There, I told you this selection would surprise you. Barry is the choice here not only for his NBA Hall of Fame qualifications, but also because he excelled at three other major sports: tennis, golf and baseball. Nobody else on this list stood out in four major sports.

The seven major sports, with emphasis on the word *major*, are basketball, football, baseball, hockey, soccer, tennis and golf

The closest to Barry's four were John Havlicek, a three-sport star in high school who was good enough to play in the NFL as well as the NBA, and Bo Jackson, who was a standout in both the NFL and Major League Baseball. Film of Jackson playing basketball indicates that he had NBA potential as well: *Bo Knows Hoops!*. But to him football and baseball were the No. 1 and No. 2 sports.

These are the ten:

1. Barry.
2. Jackson.
3. Havlicek.
4. Otto Graham.
5. Hakeem Olajuwon.
6. Wilt Chamberlain

7. Michael Jordan.
8. Oscar Robertson.
9. Julius Erving.
10. Dominique Wilkins.

Now, about those four sports in which Barry has excelled. A great clutch player, he is the career American Basketball Association record holder, having averaged 30.5 points per game for his four seasons in the league. He is also the career post-season record-holder with 33.5 points per game.

His NBA highlights include averaging 28.2 points in a championship series. He was named MVP. He is the only player ever to lead the NCAA, NBA and ABA in scoring for full seasons. His 37.4 average was tops in the NCAA during his senior year at the University of Miami.

Barry also got hot, pouring in 38 points in an upset victory by the West over the East in the 1967 NBA All-Star Game. It was the only time Oscar Robertson played for the losing side in the 12 games in which he participated.

A dreadful mistake by the New York Knicks probably cost them several NBA titles. During their two NBA championship seasons, which occurred while Barry was in his prime, they had Bill Bradley playing small forward.

Bradley was the solitary weak link in the Knicks' starting lineup with scoring, rebounding and assists stats all below average for the small forward position. His career TENDEX rating was .403, about 100 percentage points below average for a starting small forward in the NBA.

A Knicks fan at that time, I had seen both Barry and Bradley play in college and was horrified when they picked Bradley No. 1 in 1965. I had seen him decisively outplayed the year before by an AAU player in the 1964 Olympic trials.

I mention this because the Knicks selected Bradley No. 1 in the 1965 draft when they could have taken Barry. Barry, who grew up in New Jersey not far from New York City, was a Knicks fan who wanted to play for the New York team. His across-the-board PAR numbers for his entire NBA career nearly doubled those of Bradley.

With Barry in the lineup instead of Bradley, the Knicks might have won as many as a half-dozen titles between 1965 and 1975 and Barry could have stayed with that team instead of leaving San Francisco and moving to the ABA to play in his home city with the New York Nets. He led one team to an ABA championship before returning to the NBA and leading Golden State to a title in what was considered an upset.

The next chapter, about the NBA draft, will feature a multitude of inexplicable errors by NBA scouts just as bad as the one favoring Bradley, a one-dimensional player, over Barry, who did just about everything well and could have filled the one huge hole the Nets had in a lineup that included All-Stars Willis Reed, Jerry Lucas, Walt Frazier and Dave DeBusschere.

A lot of New Yorkers have contended (without statistical support) that one of the two Knicks' teams that won NBA titles was the best team ever in the NBA. Actually, neither of those teams was close to the best, according to the TENDEX formula for rating teams.

But replacing Bradley with Barry would have given the Nets almost an invincible lineup. The Knicks might, indeed, have placed on the court the greatest team of all-time during the prime decade of Rick Barry.

In the first NBA game in which Barry and Bradley were matched up head-to-head, Barry embarrassed the team that had overlooked him the draft. He scored 57 points, made 21 of 22 free throws, and pulled down 15 rebounds.

So, in addition to being a so-so offensive player you can get an idea from this at how truly awful Bradley was on defense.

To my knowledge, Bradley did not himself achieve any of the single-game numbers he gave up to Barry in their first NBA meeting a single time during his entire NBA career. Those totals were about normal by Bradley for a sequence of four games, not one.

It is almost a sure thing that a Knick team with a starting lineup containing so much talent would have shortened the dynasty of the Auerbach-coached Celtics by couple of seasons, even though Lucas did not join the team until later.

Besides basketball and tennis, Barry also was a good golfer and baseball player. In fact, baseball was his No. 1 sport in his early teens. But by the time he was a high school senior, basketball had taken over.

"We had a lot of thirty-twenty games," his brother Dennis said in reference to the high school scoring and rebounding totals of both brothers. An injury thwarted Dennis Barry's basketball ambitions, but a close family member said Dennis had possessed as much basketball potential as Rick.

More than five decades after high school graduation, at a time in life when most men are losing strength and agility, Rick Barry won a contest by driving a golf ball 350 yards.

IS THERE ANYTHING BO DON'T KNOW?

Bo Jackson, No. 2 on the list above, was an All-Pro running back in the NFL with a career rushing average of 6.6 yards per carry. That average reflected the unusual combination of power and speed that Jackson possessed.

He demonstrated both traits at Auburn University and won the Heisman Trophy. He also played college baseball.

His NFL career was ended by a hip injury, and he turned to Major League Baseball. After a slow start, he began to demonstrate power comparable to any other major leaguer at that time. He was closing in on 40 home runs late one season when bad luck struck again.

While diving in an effort to catch a short fly ball, he damaged a shoulder so badly that he was forced to stop playing baseball. He didn't play in the NBA but in my opinion he could have. He was one of the two greatest athletes I ever saw.

The other was Mickey Mantle, who hit the longest home runs and had the fastest time to first base of any player in MLB history. Without substance-assistance of any kind, Mantle compiled the most home runs and

RBIs in World Series history. He helped the Yankees win 12 pennants and seven Series.

Jackson had that kind of potential, the only man I ever saw who was as strong and, well, *almost* as fast as Mantle.

A three-sport standout in high school, John Havlicek still had a choice between two of them after college. He could have played in either the NFL or the NBA. It did not surprise me that he chose the side of one if the world's most persuasive talkers, Red Auerbach, and joined the Celtics instead of the Cleveland Browns. The Browns had been looking at him to play the wide receiver position.

Havlicek was an NBA All-Star for 13 consecutive seasons between 1966 and 1978. A steal of his after a turnover by Bill Russell saved one of 11 titles the Celtics won during the tenure of Russell.

Russell praised Havlicek, calling him "the best all-around ball player I ever saw."

Havlicek played on six of the dynastic Auerbach teams, but his noteworthy performances were in leading Boston later to two titles with much less talent during the mid-1970s, for a total of eight. He was the finals MVP in 1974.

He is the Celtics' all-time leading scorer and has balanced that offense with eight citations for All-NBA Defensive teams.

The Cleveland Browns believed he had similar football potential if he had chosen to play in the NFL.

A GREAT BROWN NOT NAMED JIM

A versatile athlete who fulfilled his greatness in 10 seasons with the Browns was Otto Graham. With Graham at quarterback the Browns won four straight titles in the All-American Football Conference.

Then, after other NFL teams were fattened up by players added from the defunct AAFC, the Browns continued to dominate. They won three NFL titles during the next six seasons and reached the finals in the three they did not win.

With Graham at QB, the Browns set an NFL winning percentage record for those seasons six seasons (.810). Graham also set a record that still stands with an average of 8.63 yards per passing attempt.

In TENDEX ratings for NFL quarterbacks, Graham ranks among the top three of all-time along with Steve Young and Tom Brady. Graham is the only quarterback of the post-World War II era to be ranked among the all-time NFL leaders.

He was also an excellent basketball player, who could have played in the NBA. He helped the Rochester Royals win a National Basketball League title in 1945-46.

He became the first athlete to play for two title-winning teams in major professional sports in the same year, because 1946 was the first year he led the Browns to an AAFC championship.

The Royals joined the NBA right after winning the NBL title, but Graham decided to play NFL football after that.

The other six players on the top-ten list of versatile athletes all had less obvious credentials. As far as I know, the final two, Erving and Wilkins, excelled in basketball only. But both had immense athleticism. In a final-four standing high jump competition, I'd predict victory for Erving and Wilkins over Michael Jordan and LeBron James, great leapers who have had superior NBA careers.

But Erving and Wilkins had great careers, too. Erving totaled more than 30,000 career points combined in the NBA and ABA. This came after he was drafted only No. 12 in 1972 by the Milwaukee Bucks, which once again suggests something has been seriously wrong with the judgment of NBA scouts.

The remaining four were known (at least by this author) to have had great potential in at least one sport other than basketball. By the way, all four, not just Jordan, were outstanding leapers.

We have mentioned Chamberlain's extraordinary free-throw dunk. He was also a world-class quarter-miler. He might have qualified for the 1960 Olympic Games in the broad jump or the quarter-mile. But how he applied his track-and-field abilities to his basketball game was the bottom line for him. In those days they did not allow NBA players to compete in the Olympic Games, which at that time was still considered an amateur sporting event.

It was a similar story for Hakeem Olajuwon. After a slow start in training to become a soccer goalkeeper, he developed post-to-post range in defending the soccer goal. The ability he acquired to lunge and/or dive in any direction to prevent a goal was of value to him when he changed sports and became a basketball player. Like Chamberlain, Olajuwon made the one (soccer goalkeeping) into a tool for excelling in the other (blocking shots and boxing out for position for rebounds).

An NBA Hall of Famer, he is remembered best for leading the Houston Rockets to league titles in both of the seasons between the two streaks of three titles in a row by the Chicago Bulls. Olajuwon was league MVP in both seasons and dominated New York Knicks rival Patrick Ewing in playoff series both years.

For pure athleticism it is difficult to outdo Jordan. Besides out-jumping most opponents in basketball situations, he was at one time (during "retirement") a professional baseball player for a minor league team.

Robertson is listed No. 8 after guys who played well in at least two sports and before guys who were single-minded when it came to athletic participation. By now, the reader is aware of the author's opinion that Robertson was unexcelled on a basketball floor.

Here's another opinion: Robertson could have become great in almost any sport of his choosing. Let's stick with America's favorite three and discuss his potential in two sports, football and baseball.

While working two years in Cincinnati as a sportswriter, I heard talk that Robertson had as much potential to play the quarterback position as anybody. I gave it some thought and, yes, his intelligence and leadership were first-rate as are those of NFL quarterbacks.

Another thing was he could throw a basketball 30 yards, from one end of the court to the other, into the hands of a teammate comparable to an NFL wide receiver: Perfect pass and two points most of the time. Consider what he might have done with a football designed specifically to be thrown.

Improvisation, at which Robertson excelled as an NBA point guard, also is important for a quarterback, who must make split-second decisions after the ball is snapped. At 6-foot-5 and a rock-solid 225 pounds, there was no doubt about Robertson's athleticism. If he didn't make it as an NFL quarterback, he might have found a place in the NFL as a hard-hitting linebacker or a tight end.

But the thing I'll never forget was, perhaps, the only time Robertson swung a baseball bat before a packed house. It was Crosley Field, home of the Cincinnati Reds, and I can't recall the occasion or even all of the participants. But part of the agenda for the day was to give Robertson a chance to take at least one swing.

As it turned out, one was all he needed.

I remember joining with thousands of others in good-natured smiles when the large (they didn't call him the Big O for no reason) Robertson picked up a bat and carefully placed his left hand more than one inch from the end. This is called choking up. It is not a bad thing, but is not often done by macho baseball players.

Robertson did it.

On the first pitch, at batting practice speed, Robertson took a swing so well coordinated that it looked as if it could have been done only by a great baseball player like Frank Robinson, at that time a star for the Reds. The sound of bat meeting ball was a click, known by players to be the noise accompanying the hardest-hit balls.

Not a crack, but a click.

The ball flew off Robertson's bat on a line toward right-center field about ten or twelve feet above the ground. It hit the right-centerfield field fence on one bounce about 375 feet from home plate.

Yes, it was a batting practice pitch, the easiest to hit. But the pitch didn't have enough velocity for a hitter simply make contact and expect it to carry *that* far. The batter had to supply the power. And, in this case, to the opposite field, the ball had been hit hard enough to carry far over the fence if it had been 25 feet above ground instead of ten.

The trajectory of that ball reminded me of a line drive off the bat of Robinson. It was a bullet, and Robertson did not even appear to be swinging hard. It was hit harder than any ball I had seen hit by Jordan in two years of minor league baseball covered nearly every day by TV's Sports Center programming.

It happened nearly 60 years ago, and I remember it as well as some of the the best shots I saw off the bat of Mickey Mantle.

It was much harder hit than any ball I had seen hit by Pete Rose during my full-season coverage of Reds' home games or even pre-game batting practice.

So who's doubting Oscar Robertson's athletic versatility?

CHAPTER ELEVEN

MOST AMAZING FACT ABOUT NBA SCOUTS

Some people think that, as creator of TENDEX, I can influence the statistics that the system produces and slant them toward personal opinion. This may be true of some statisticians, but not me.

More often than not, TENDEX has humbled me. This has happened when players I rated highest for the draft from personal observation were shoved forward or backward by their actual performance in the NBA.

TENDEX has proved more accurate than my observations most of the time and has sustained an even greater advantage over the NBA scouting system. All I have to do is listen for about 30 seconds to raving comments by a scout or media "expert" about a player's "wingspan" and I feel like regurgitating my latest meal.

Why not just tell me if the guy can play? That's what I want to know, and it's what TENDEX does better than any team's scouting system that I know about. A few teams' front office personnel have done a good job on their own of rating players for one or two drafts with minimal help from scouts. I know because they told me they wanted to see some TENDEX arithmetic.

I recall a conversation in which Don Nelson and I discussed the potential of Latrell Sprewell as an NBA player. Nelson liked him. I had seen Sprewell play college basketball and remembered him as a good all-around player. I checked some TENDEX numbers and told Nelson I thought Sprewell could play in the NBA at both ends of the floor.

Nelson drafted him near the bottom of the first round. A perimeter player, he went on to average 18.3 points per game for a 13-year NBA career. During his five peak seasons his scoring average was 21.2.

What a steal!

HOW TO WIN NBA TITLES

I have often said that if a team wants to win NBA titles, all it has to do is rate players according to TENDEX and try to sign the highest rated. I know that because TENDEX ratings are better than mine almost every time. And so, when I participate in draft games, as I have done for a half-century, I compute TENDEX ratings for the players and make nearly all of my selections based on those ratings.

Here's an example: In 2009, TENDEX rated James Harden No. 1 and Stephen Curry No. 2 overall for the NBA draft. I thought it possible that if I made the well-publicized Curry my first selection, Harden might be available at No. 2.

Since in that game I was opposed by only one player, I thought he would be more likely to overlook Harden than Curry, because Curry appeared to be more highly rated than Harden and, therefore, more publicized by most of the numerous draft-projection systems.

But I choked. I took Harden and my game opponent chose Curry, as I feared he would. He told me that if I had taken Curry first, he would not have picked Harden.

My bad!

Those two have emerged as the top players from that draft and are sure future Hall of Famers, with Harden rating at the moment as the No. 5 player of all-time, according to TENDEX.

Curry is a bit farther down in the NBA ratings of TENDEX and three other systems I am familiar with.

I was correct (thanks to TENDEX) on Harden. My friend was correct in picking Curry, his No. 1 choice, at No. 2 when he had the chance.

Bottom line; TENDEX outperformed all of the publicized scouting systems by correctly rating Harden and Curry 1-2.

Now for the NBA scouts: Since they selected Harden with the No. 3 choice in that draft and Curry at No. 7, it's clear that they messed up on both men.

Here's the amazing fact referred to in the title of this chapter: During a span between 1984 and 2003, TENDEX graded out better overall than the scouts in 18 of the 20 drafts. The first draft rated by TENDEX was 1984, so this is not a fact carefully picked out from the midst of contradictory evidence. These were the first 20 drafts to be rated according to TENDEX.

I repeat: There were no TENDEX-rated drafts before 1984, the year TENDEX was introduced to the general public by means of a weekly column appearing in *Basketball Times*.

The reader does not need to know how to compute TENDEX ratings in order to check this out. All he/she has to do is compare NBA careers of these key players with their placement in drafts in which they were selected during those 20 years. At that time a comparison can be made with these players' published TENDEX ratings.

In most of the years in question, this was not a close contest.

There were some players about whom TENDEX and the scouts agreed should be No. 1, but there were a lot of draft bloopers by the scouts. These were a few of the most flagrant ones involving No. 1 choices:

- Derrick Coleman over Gary Payton (No. 2) in 1990.
- Larry Johnson over Dikembe Mutombo (4) in 1991.
- Glenn Robinson over Jason Kidd (2) and Grant Hill (3) in 1994.
- Joe Smith over Kevin Garnett (5) in 1995.
- Allen Iverson over Kobe Bryant (13) in 1996.
- Michael Olowokandi over Dirk Nowitzki (9) in 1998.
- Kwame Brown over Pau Gasol (3) in 2001.

All of the players on the above list who were drafted below No. 1 became Hall of Famers. Only one drafted No. 1, Allen Iverson, did the same. And Iverson was not anywhere near as good as Kobe Bryant, who was drafted 12 places beneath him. Because of intangibles such as weak man defense, it was a close call whether

Iverson should be among the top 75 players of all-time as chosen by TENDEX for this book. Bryant is among the top dozen.

I did a chart for a book I co-wrote entitled *Basic Ball* in 2011. In that chart were listed outstanding players who had been drafted correctly by TENDEX and those who were draft winners for the scouts. Some outstanding players are omitted from this list because they were No. 1 choices of both TENDEX and the scouts.

The original TENDEX victory list cited seven players for every three on the scouts' list. TENDEX winners included Michael Jordan, Hakeem Olajuwon, John Stockton, Charles Barkley, Mark Price, Reggie Miller, Mark Jackson, Gary Payton, Chris Mullin, Tim Hardaway, Dikembe Mutombo, Penny Hardaway, Steve Nash, Vince Carter, Paul Pierce, Shawn Marion, Caron Butler and Dwyane Wade. The names of James Harden and Steph Curry were later added to this list.

Most noteworthy winners for the scouts have been Kevin Johnson, Mitch Richmond, Mookie Blaylock, Grant Hill, Donyell Marshall, Jerry Stackhouse, Stephon Marbury, Chris Bosh, Deron Williams and Al Horford.

If these two rosters competed against each other in a series of games, with all players in their primes, which do you think would win? Do you think the TENDEX second team could defeat the scouts' best?

THE GREATEST DRAFT

On the list of outstanding TENDEX draft choices above, the first four players named were selected in the

1984 draft, which, after their first few NBA seasons could be rated, turned out to be the best draft of all-time.

The 1960 draft, featuring Oscar Robertson, Jerry West and Walt Bellamy, was close behind. But the 1984 draft was deeper than then 1960 draft. Besides the top four, all of whom are rated by TENDEX among the top 75 players of all-time, there were other excellent players who had long NBA careers: Alvin Robertson (No. 7 choice by the scouts), Otis Thorpe (No. 9), Kevin Willis (11), Michael Cage (14), Vern Fleming (18) and Jerome Kersey (46).

It is perhaps an odd coincidence that this was the first year in which TENDEX ratings were computed for draft-available players.

It could not be done before then for a good reason: It was necessary to ascertain strength of schedule ratings for every team that played the teams played for by players selected in this draft. This was a daunting task, which became easier through the years when a season-by-season consistency was observed in the schedule strengths of most college teams.

It is much easier for a player to put up large numbers for his team if the opponent is weak. The converse obviously also is true. Top-to-bottom difference in team strength is about 30%. What a difference that can make in a TENDEX rating.

As far as I know, nobody else has done the schedule-strength work necessary to compute accurate ratings for college players. A much easier task, but also an important one, was the retrospective computation of ratings for these players in earlier collegiate seasons.

Rate-of-improvement was a factor in deciding that Jordan was potentially a better player than Olajuwon and that Stockton was likely to wind up, as he did, the next best player after those two. Stockton and Barkley had almost identical TENDEX ratings for their final seasons in college; but the large improvement-rate advantage should have given Stockton the final edge as a draft choice.

Three statistical systems other than TENDEX that rated the two players for their NBA careers, all gave Stockton the edge.

Stockton, as mentioned earlier in this book, was the dominant player in a decisive conference championship game in which the desperate Barkley knocked him down three times in an apparent effort to force him to take a seat on the bench.

Yes, Stockton, who, like Robertson and Harden, sometimes has had bogus criticism mounted against him by supporters of other players, has been a better NBA player than the ever-popular TV-commentator, Charles Barkley.

Both players were good enough to be No. 1 choices in most drafts.

Stockton's No. 16 choice in the 1984 draft was inexplicable.

HUMBLED BY THE STATS

A lot of people think that, as creator of TENDEX, I can influence the statistics that the system produces and slant them toward personal opinion. This is probably true of a lot of statisticians, but not me.

More often than not, TENDEX humbles me. This has happened at draft time when players I rated highest from personal observation were shoved forward or backward by their actual performance in the NBA.

TENDEX has proved more accurate than my observations most of the time and has maintained about the same edge over the NBA scouting system.

The front offices of a few teams have done a good job on their own of rating players for one or two drafts with minimal help from scouts. I know because they asked me to do the arithmetic.

I have often said that if a team wants to win NBA titles, all its statistician needs to do is use TENDEX formulae to run some numbers and choose players through drafts and trades based on those numbers.

One franchise that has never won a title probably had that in mind when it offered to hire the TENDEX inventor full-time, but it couldn't be worked out. I think that, if it had been arranged, this team probably would have won several titles with the help of TENDEX player ratings.

CHAPTER TWELVE

FILLING IN THE BLANKS

TENDEX was the first globally-used basketball statistical system and, I think, also, the best of them all. I'm told that the big thing right now is analytics. So how come the encyclopedia mentioned earlier in this book used a TENDEX formula instead of analytics for its player database?

No system is perfect. It has been proved true that the average NBA ball possession produces an average of about one point. This makes TENDEX easy to compute and accurate. Each item (a point, rebound, assist or ball-possession change) is either plus-one point or minus-one. The exception that always has disturbed me is the assisted basket. In that case TENDEX is awarding three points for a play resulting in only two points.

But it's the only fair way. The player who scores a field goal gets two points (or three, for a three point shot). Player who found the shooter with a key pass gets an assist, one point. His pass has turned a normal one-point ball possession into a two-pointer.

After having been told how prevalent so-called analytics has become, I found out something about it recently that brought laughter. The new system, or at least version of it I heard about, awards four points for a two-point basket. Playmaker and scorer receive two points each. So the total for a three-point basket is five. Wow! Five points for a single basket.

That's about equivalent to a 50-foot shot.

I'm not sure what the rationale is for this, but, whatever it is, does not compute: I have had enough trouble explaining to myself how a two-point basket can be valued at three points.

But four points?

Let's not be ridiculous.

John Harris is a long-time friend who for many years did most of the work on the annual TENDEX draft reports, which were of course more accurate than the body of work done by an array of well-paid scouts. Despite the extra point for assisted baskets, TENDEX remains the system to use, according to Harris.

He said this recently: "Prior to the 2006 NBA Draft, Dave (Heeren) slapped a top-10 draft rating on some player I had never heard of, Paul Millsap from Louisiana Tech. Instead of questioning his logic, I looked at Dave's track record over the years and kept my mouth shut. Utah selected Millsap late in the second round with the 47th overall pick. Millsap became an All-Star who has earned well over $100 million in his career.

"I guarantee you that Dave Heeren was the only scout in America who knew that Millsap was a special player. Clearly, no NBA team knew how good he was; otherwise, he wouldn't have lasted as long as he did. As far as I am concerned, all of these so-called scouting gurus and draftniks are stealing money. They can't hold a candle to Dave Heeren, the OG of basketball analytics."

Personal pride aside, I have a confession to make: TENDEX beats my personal draft selections – with TENDEX ratings omitted – by just as wide a margin as it beats the scouts. In this case, the system is much smarter than its inventor.

Nevertheless, thanks for the good word, John.

FOUR MEN OF STRONG CHARACTER

Before posting official TENDEX numbers on the four greatest players, I'd like to engage in a bit of nostalgia with a few comments about them. These give strong evidence favoring the idea that all four were/are men of strong character:

MICHAEL JORDAN: Always a great athlete with exceptional vertical leap and basketball instincts, Jordan became revered quickly in the NBA. But it was not until his third season that he matured as a player and not until his eighth that his team won an NBA title. His rate of improvement through college and his first few NBA seasons was off the charts. Most players enjoying such reverence would sit back and wallow around in it. Not Jordan. He worked at improving his game. He was a pure shooting guard at first, without many ball-controlling skills other than a crossover dribble that often could have drawn a whistle from a referee as a carry/turnover. But by the time he returned from his first retirement he was a complete player. Not as great an athlete as he once had been, but making up for it with new skills acquired through hard work.

WILT CHAMBERLAIN: I learned much about Wilt in an interview one year before his death. It was at a basketball camp for handicapped boys that he was sponsoring at a gym in Boca Raton, FL. Throughout the day, he spent most of his time signing items that were to be presented to camp participants. I was aware of Wilt's great physical strength, even late in life. But I noticed the time he spent and the care he exercised in signing each item. The man, known to be one of the most powerful in NBA history, had artistic talent. We discussed a lot of things. He told me that the MVP he earned for leading the Los Angeles Lakers to an NBA title with himself also Championship Finals MVP in 1972, the year before he retired, was achieved with two broken hands. Before I left for the day, he gestured around the gym and said to me: "Why don't you do a story about these kids?"

LeBRON JAMES: With free agency year not far away, at the Olympics in 2008, James demonstrated a character trait few NBA players possess: The ability to make a personal choice without allowing money and/or prestige to be decisive. He chose his next teammate/friend carefully: Dwyane Wade, who was statistically the best player in those Games. While Los Angeles fans were hoping he would pick Kobe Bryant and sign with the Lakers, New York fans were believing it would be the Knicks and Carmelo Anthony. Both teams were disappointed. But James had what he wanted: A Miami team that, in four years featuring Wade and himself, reached the Championship Finals all four times, won two of them, and didn't win a third only because of a three-game losing streak resulting from performance-affecting injuries to both players. James did not play at all for a major-market team (Los Angeles) until his 16th season in the NBA.

OSCAR ROBERTSON: Despite a basketball career beginning with a display of world-class talent while he was still in high school, things have not always gone well for the Big O. This was especially true of the pre-NBA season when he wanted to tour with the Harlem Globetrotters. The year before, Chamberlain had become a Globetrotter for $60,000. The Globetrotters offered Robertson $17,000. He turned it down. Why should he be offered so much less money than Chamberlain when he was a perfect fit for the Trotters? He could dunk two basketballs, while palming a ball in each hand, on a single leap. He had dribbling and ball-handling skills comparable to legendary Globetrotter Marques Haynes. But when it was about his family, personal pride was not a factor. When his daughter contracted an illness that caused life-threatening degeneration of the kidneys, her father gave her one of his. Asked about it later, he said: "What father would not do that for his daughter?"

FINAL WORD ABOUT FIVE GREAT PLAYERS

Of the NBA players in upper echelons of stardom, the most difficult ones to assess were Bill Russell and Oscar Robertson. The two had parallel careers and wound up playing for less prominent colleges than Wilt Chamberlain's Kansas.

Russell dominated the 1956 Olympic Games with his defense, especially shot-blocking. Robertson dominated the 1960 Olympics with his all-around superlative performance.

Both men were held in awe by Olympians from all over the world. Robertson became a featured speaker at informal clinics given by the U.S. team. These were requested by awed opponents in 1960.

In Russell's case, knowing what an impactful defensive player he was, we generously added steals and blocked shots to the researched numbers (the NBA did not record them during his career).

In Robertson's case, we left the stats as they were, upholding the computed rating based on known numbers. But I am confident that Russell's numbers, like Robertson's, were not overrated because Russell was such a big-play defender.

We recorded what seemed to be a reasonable number of turnovers, steals and blocks for Wilt Chamberlain (less steals and blocks than Russell), so I think Chamberlain's original TENDEX value rating number (+57.7) also is accurate, at least at that point.

For Robertson's first six seasons in the NBA, his TENDEX value rating was above the "superstar" minimum of +60%. Actually, the six averaged out to over +70% with a high of +89.1%, by far the best single-season rating for any player in NBA history.

Based on evidence that he was as good as a college sophomore – when he should have been allowed to play in the NBA, but was not – as he was as an NBA rookie, it seems that +75% probably was a more accurate figure for his performance during his peak decade than the listed +58.6%.

Support for this statement comes from a comparison between the careers of Robertson and LeBron James, who, according to John Wooden, was the second-best high school player of all-time, behind Robertson.

When James was in high school, NBA rules allowed him to be drafted into the league. He was the No. 1 choice and after earning Rookie-of-the-Year honors strung together eight straight seasons when he led the league in TENDEX rating.

This was tied for the most with Jordan.

But the relevant fact here is that in the three seasons when Robertson would have been a sophomore, junior and senior in college he was so clearly in a class by himself that we are left with little doubt that he would have been the NBA's best player in all three. His primary competition at that time were Russell and Bopb Pettit, neither of whom was close to Robertson in all-around basketball skills.

Coupled with a great freshman season paralleling James' Rookie of the Year performance, it seems clear that Robertson's true peak decade of performance included the four collegiate seasons. In replacement for the lesser seasons that were counted later on, this would have given him about a 20% edge over the other three great players, instead of the single point edge he is credited with below.

Robertson would have been the TENDEX honoree as best player nine times during that decade, instead of the six he was rewarded with. And his year-to-year ratings were better than the best of James and Jordan.

Chamberlain did post better ratings than Robertson five times, but those were mostly in seasons after Robertson's prime. These are not included in Robertson's adjusted prime decade.

The rating below omits the major issues listed above, including the speculative, but evidential one, supporting the idea that Robertson was the best player in the world during his last three years of college, and maybe all four..

INFLATION OR DEFLATION?

If you think he is being overrated, here is one more thing. There is no chance that Robertson's No. 1 TENDEX rating of all-time based on official numbers (at the end of this chapter) for NBA players were inflated.

They were deflated.

Playing in a league with about one-third as many teams as in the best decades of Jordan and James, Robertson and also Chamberlain compiled statistics so good that their own value ratings were reduced.

This is because a positional norm or average is included in the TENDEX formula, and this norm was increased more by the ratings of Robertson and Chamberlain, with many fewer players in the mix, than those of Jordan and James.

The best TENDEX ratings are based on comparisons with norms. The higher the norm, the lower the player rating.

In a strange, but real way, these players' high ratings caused the overall league average for their position to be increased significantly. This was more evident in a nine-team league (Robertson, Chamberlain) than one with 27 or more (Jordan, James).

It is known that Robertson's assists were reduced by more than any other NBA player of his era, even though he led the league officially eight times. If the computations had been accurate, in the four years when he was feeding Kareem Abdul-Jabbar for baskets six or seven times a game for what were ruled unassisted baskets, it would have been 12 assists titles instead of eight for the Big O.

Robertson's final four seasons were actually his best for assists. But, according to official league stats, they were his worst. That's because, as I understand it, the league instructed statisticians not to count as assists any passes to players with their backs to the basket.

Whether or not it was based on instructions from the NBA office, official scorers in all league cities but one did not award assists for such passes.

Abdul-Jabbar was by far the best NBA center with ability to receive a pass with his back to the basket, turn and toss in a short hook shot.

But these, according to the NBA, were unassisted baskets.

PRIME RATINGS FOR ROBERTSON

The prime decade ratings for Robertson, unlike the other three players, were his last three at the University of Cincinnati. For him these should be included because they were within his prime decade of performance – an essential factor.

It is incontrovertible that Robertson was a much better player for the UC varsity than he was in the NBA after his seventh season.

The following numbers are as accurate as possible. When in doubt, the smaller number has been used. For instance, a lot of evidence indicated Robertson's rating should be as high as +75.0 or even higher.

His and Chamberlain's ratings have been adjusted on the basis of relevant statistical information in addition to TENDEX. However, the Hall of Fame chart at the end of this book has not been changed.

Here are the final prime-decade TENDEX value ratings for the NBA's greatest players. Years included for Robertson are 1958-67 instead of 1961-70.

The order of placement of the top four players has not changed, but the space between them has widened:

1. Oscar Robertson……..+73.0.
2. Wilt Chamberlain……+60.0
3. LeBron James………..+56.1

    4.   Michael Jordan.........+55.5

FUTURE LEADERS?

   Giannis Antetokounmpo – I call him Topo – appears to be a developing NBA superstar. He has achieved TENDEX value ratings of +49.8, +53.6 and +40.0 the past three seasons, averaging +47.8 for the three. Led Milwaukee to a league championship in 2020-21. Second-place finisher behind James Harden for TENDEX MVP in 2018-19 and 2019-20

   Two other young players also aspire to NBA greatness: Nikola Jokic of Denver, the TENDEX 2020-21 Player of the Year with a rating of +49.8, and Luka Doncic of Dallas, who placed second at +41.3.

   Others envisioning stardom include Ben Simmons, Joel Embiid, Domantas Sabonis, Bradley Beal and Rudy Gobert

Statistical NBA Hall of Fame

(Minimum 20,000 Minutes Played)

Player	Seasons	Pos.	Norm	TEN.	M/Sea	Value
1. Oscar Robertson	1961-70	PG	.465	.797	3,307	+58.6
2. Wilt Chamberlain	1960-69	C	.615	.993	3,671	+57.7
3. LeBron James	2005-14	SF	.487	.849	3,010	+56.1
4. Michael Jordan	1987-97	G	.469	.841	2,911	+55.5
5. James Harden	2012-21	G	.461	.795	2,751	+48.4
6. Kevin Durant	2009-19	SF .	466	.783	2,762	+46.2
7. David Robinson	1990-00	C	.535	.876	2,777	+42.1
8. K. Abdul-Jabbar	1971-80	C	.591	.930	3,138	+41.3
9. Karl Malone	1989-98	PF	.532	.822	3,130	+40.1
10. Larry Bird	1980-90	SF	.497	.772	3,032	+39.1
11. Hakeem Olajuwon	1987-96	C	.522	.834	2,860	+38.9
12. Dwyane Wade	2005-15	SG	.446	.747	2,421	+37.6
13. Kevin Garnett	1999-08	PF/C	.549	.853	2,935	+37.4
14. Magic Johnson	1982-91	PG	.471	.767	2,812	+37.0
15. Kobe Bryant	2000-10	SG	.457	.701	2,948	+35.7
16. Bob Pettit	1955-64	PF	.548	.822	2,894	+34.9
17. Tim Duncan	2000-09	F/C	.554	.854	2,797	+34.3
18. Russell Westbrook	2011-21	PG	.475	.715	2,586	+34.2
19. Chris Paul	2007-16	PG	.484	.758	2,601	+33.9
20. Bill Russell	1960-69	C	.612	.845	3,341	+33.4
21. Patrick Ewing	1988-97	C	.525	.788	2,943	+33.2
22. Shaquille O'Neal	1994-03	C	.544	.867	2,496	+32.3
23. John Stockton	1988-97	PG	.485	.720	2,954	+32.2
24. Charles Barkley	1986-95	PF	.523	.790	2,795	+32.1
25. Julius Erving	1973-82	F	.497	.726	2,968	+30.6
26. Jerry West	1964-73	G	.474	.707	2,756	+29.6
27. Clyde Drexler `	1986-95	SG	.452	.670	2,683	+28.8
28. John Havlicek	1966-75	G/F	.454	.593	3,121	+27.7
29. Stephen Curry	2013-21*	PG	.492	.716	2,487	+27.2

30. Tracy McGrady	1999-08	G/F	.463	.689	2,510	+25.9
31. George Gervin	1974-83	G/F	.449	.639	2,817	+25.9
32. Jerry Lucas	1964-73	PF	.550	.741	3,050	+24.4
33. Jason Kidd	1999-08	PG	.475	.672	2,749	+24.3
34. Paul Pierce	2000-09	F/G	.468	.646	2,889	+23.9
35. Rick Barry	1966-76	SF	.499	.656	2,784	+23.7
36. Vince Carter	2000-09	G/F	.459	.642	2,751	+23.2
37. Scottie Pippen	1991-00	SF	.475	.650	2,740	+22.7
38. Dirk Nowitzki	2001-10	PF`	.558	.753	2,983	+22.5
39. Elgin Baylor	1960-69	PF	.568	.761	2,850	+22.1
40. Moses Malone	1980-89	C	.545	.733	2,955	+21.8
41. Walt Frazier	1969-78	PG	.468	.624	2,900	+21.4
42. Gary Payton	1994-03	PG	.481	.628	3,060	+20.7
43. Artis Gilmore	1973-82	C	.586	.754	3,142	+19.5
44. Elton Brand	2000-07*	PF	.556	.729	2,903	+18.7
45. Steve Nash	2002-11	PG	.475	.641	2,663	+18.4
46. Dominique Wilkins	1985-94	SF	.487	.639	2,784	+17.7
47. Shawn Marion	2000-09	F	.506	.664	2,802	+17.6
48. Larry Nance	1983-92	F	.496	.667	2,585	+17.3
49. Bob McAdoo	1973-80*	C/PF	.569	.732	2,865	+17.1
50. Elvin Hayes	1969-78	F/C	.546	.678	3.337	+17.0
51. Shawn Kemp	1991-00	PF	.538	.716	2,423	+16.9
52. Dwight Howard	2005-14	C/PF	.575	.750	2,759	+16.8
53. Ray Allen	2000-07*	SG	.458	.593	2,758	+15.8
54. Carmelo Anthony	2005-14	F	.488	.642	2,584	+15.5
55. Sam Cassell	1998-06*	PG	.473	.625	2,566	+15.4
56. Bob Lanier	1991-00	C	.591	.781	2,538	+15.3
57. Alonzo Mourning	1993-02	C	.543	.748	2,180	+15.1
58. Sam Jones	1959-68	SG	.437	.578	2,187	+14.6
59. Reggie Miller	1990-99	SG	.448	.558	2,771	+14.4
60. Dikembe Mutombo	1993-02	C	.543	.685	2,790	+14.3
61. Dennis Rodman	1988-97	F	.516	.682	2,378	+14.3
62. Allen Iverson	1999-08	G	.467	.587	2,843	+14.3
63. Sidney Moncrief	1980-89#	SG	.450	.593	2,106	+14.0

64. Bill Cunningham	1967-76	F	.519	.686	2,471	+13.7
65. Kevin McHale	1982-91	PF	.512	.658	2,542	+13.7
66. Robert Parish	1981-90	C	.531	.681	2,612	+13.5
67. Adrian Dantley	1977-87	SF	.496	.617	2,727	+13.4
68. Isiah Thomas	1983-92	PG	.474	.584	2,841	+13.1
69. Walter Davis	1978-88	G/F	.460	.601	2,257	+12.6
70. Hal Greer	1961-70	SG	.441	.527	2,987	+12.5
71. Jeff Hornacek	1990-99	SG	.448	.556	2,554	+12.5
72. Kevin Johnson	1988-97	PG	.483	.629	2,366	+12.2
73. Alex English	1979-88	SF	.496	.606	2,891	+12.2
74. Chris Webber	1997-07	PF	.550	.710	2,431	+12.2
75. Richie Guerin	1957-66	G	.433	.546	2,464	+11.9

Eight seasons rated. Active players may improve career ratings with good future seasons.
 # Nine seasons rated.
Eleven seasons are indicated for many players, deleting one severely shortened by injury.
Player ratings within the decade of 1946-55 were too low for inclusion in this chart.

Honorable Mention

Minimum Rating +10.0, Descending Order

Chet Walker, Jack Sikma, Pete Maravich, Willis Reed, Detlef Schrempf, Cliff Hagan, Marques Johnson, Paul Westphal, Chauncey Billups, Connie Hawkins, Walt Bellamy, Alvin Robertson, LenWilkens, Nate (Tiny) Archibald, Terry Cummings, Tim Hardaway, George McGinnis, Dan Roundfield, Mo Cheeks, Randy Smith, Ron Boone, Rod Strickland, Bob Dandridge, Lou Hudson, Nate Thurmond, Gus Williams, Mitch Richmond, Dan Issel, Bailey Howell, Spencer Haywood, Tom Gola, Bernard King, Bill Laimbeer, George Mikan, Bob Cousy.

CPSIA information can be obtained
at www.ICGtesting.com
Printed in the USA
LVHW081729271121
704620LV00015B/1023